Frontiers in Health Policy Research 7

Frontiers in Health Policy Research 7

edited by
David M. Cutler and Alan M. Garber

National Bureau of Economic Research
Cambridge, Massachusetts

The MIT Press
Cambridge, Massachusetts
London, England

NBER/*Frontiers in Health Policy Research* Number 7, 2004
ISSN: 1531-3468
ISBN: Hardcover 0-262-03325-9
ISBN: Paperback 0-262-53266-2

Published annually by The MIT Press, Cambridge, Massachusetts 02142-1407

Standing orders/subscriptions are available. Inquiries, and changes to subscriptions and addresses should be addressed to MIT Press Standing Order Department/BB, Five Cambridge Center, Cambridge, MA 02142-1407, phone 617-258-1581, fax 617-253-1709, email standing-orders@mitpress.mit.edu

In the United Kingdom, continental Europe, and the Middle East and Africa, send single copy and back volume orders to: The MIT Press, Ltd., Fitzroy House, 11 Chenies Street, London WC1E 7ET England, phone 44-020-7306-0603, fax 44-020-7306-0604, email info@hup-MITpress.co.uk, website http://mitpress.mit.edu

In the United States and for all other countries, send single copy and back volume orders to: The MIT Press c/o Triliteral, 100 Maple Ridge Drive, Cumberland, RI 02864, phone 1-800-405-1619 (U.S. and Canada) or 401-658-4226, fax 1-800-406-9145 (U.S. and Canada) or 401-531-2801, email mitpress-orders@mit.edu, website http://mitpress.mit.edu

This book was set in Palatino 10/13 by Kolam Information Services Pvt. Ltd. and was printed and bound in the United States of America.

10 9 8 7 6 5 4 3 2 1

National Bureau of Economic Research

Relation of the Directors to the Work and Publications of the NBER

1. The object of the NBER is to ascertain and present to the economics profession, and to the public more generally, important economic facts and their interpretation in a scientific manner without policy recommendations. The Board of Directors is charged with the responsibility of ensuring that the work of the NBER is carried on in strict conformity with this object.

2. The President shall establish an internal review process to ensure that book manuscripts proposed for publication DO NOT contain policy recommendations. This shall apply both to the proceedings of conferences and to manuscripts by a single author or by one or more co-authors but shall not apply to authors of comments at NBER conferences who are not NBER affiliates.

3. No book manuscript reporting research shall be published by the NBER until the President has sent to each member of the Board a notice that a manuscript is recommended for publication and that in the President's opinion it is suitable for publication in accordance with the above principles of the NBER. Such notification will include a table of contents and an abstract or summary of the manuscript's content, a list of contributors if applicable, and a response form for use by Directors who desire a copy of the manuscript for review. Each manuscript shall contain a summary drawing attention to the nature and treatment of the problem studied and the main conclusions reached.

4. No volume shall be published until forty-five days have elapsed from the above notification of intention to publish it. During this period a copy shall be sent to any Director requesting it, and if any Director objects to publication on the grounds that the manuscript contains policy recommendations, the objection will be presented to the author(s) or editor(s). In case of dispute, all members of the Board shall be notified, and the President shall appoint an ad hoc committee of the Board to decide the matter; thirty days additional shall be granted for this purpose.

5. The President shall present annually to the Board a report describing the internal manuscript review process, any objections made by Directors before publication or by anyone after publication, any disputes about such matters, and how they were handled.

6. Publications of the NBER issued for informational purposes concerning the work of the Bureau, or issued to inform the public of the activities at the Bureau, including but not limited to the NBER Digest and Reporter, shall be consistent with the object stated in paragraph 1. They shall contain a specific disclaimer noting that they have not passed through the review procedures required in this resolution. The Executive Committee of the Board is charged with the review of all such publications from time to time.

7. NBER working papers and manuscripts distributed on the Bureau's web site are not deemed to be publications for the purpose of this resolution, but they shall be consistent with the object stated in paragraph 1. Working papers shall contain a specific disclaimer noting that they have not passed through the review procedures required in this resolution. The NBER's web site shall contain a similar disclaimer. The President shall establish an internal review process to ensure that the working papers and the web site do not contain policy recommendations, and shall report annually to the Board on this process and any concerns raised in connection with it.

8. Unless otherwise determined by the Board or exempted by the terms of paragraphs 6 and 7, a copy of this resolution shall be printed in each NBER publication as described in paragraph 2 above.

Contents

Introduction

When the seventh annual *Frontiers in Health Policy Research* meeting was held in Washington, D.C., in the summer of 2003, the climate for health care reform had decidedly changed from only a few years earlier. The projected federal budget surplus had been replaced by a budget deficit, with red ink projected to flow for the foreseeable future. Solutions to rising health expenditures seemed elusive as commercial health insurance premiums continued to rise at double-digit rates for the third consecutive year. The only major Medicare reform under serious consideration in Congress was a much-desired expansion of coverage for prescription drugs; plans to cope with rising Medicare expenditures were, for the time being, a lower priority. Along with rising health expenditures, the number of uninsured increased. The economic challenges were intense.

The papers in this volume represent some of the best thinking among leading economists about these contemporary health policy challenges. The authors, affiliated with the National Bureau of Economic Research, aim to foster a dialogue with the policy community. The papers were presented at a meeting attended by both academic researchers and health care experts within government and private organizations, and they are written for anyone concerned about the U.S. health care system and its future.

To many observers, pharmaceuticals epitomize both the successes and failures of the U.S. health care system. The rapid pace of innovation has made it possible to treat a range of conditions—such as high blood cholesterol, anemia, depression, and some cancers—more effectively than ever before. The benefits of innovation are genuine and substantial. But the medications that have been introduced for these conditions are often expensive. In recent years, pharmaceuticals have attracted a good deal of policy attention because they have comprised the leading component of health expenditure growth. Reports that residents of Canada and the wealthy nations of Europe pay less for the same drugs have fueled the debate about the fairness and sustainability of pharmaceutical markets in the United States.

Outside the United States, particularly in western Europe, reference pricing has become a popular approach to the provision of pharmaceutical benefits. The logic of reference pricing is similar to the use of tiered copayments for drugs in private health plans in the United States. A group of closely substitutable drugs is defined, and the payer (a health authority or health plan) usually adopts the price of the least expensive drug in the group as the reference price. The patient is free to choose any of the drugs in the class but must pay the difference between the drug's price and the reference price. Unlike direct price controls, this approach enables markets to function, with support for higher prices dependent on the demand for perceived superiority.

In both a theoretical analysis and an empirical examination of the effects of reference pricing in three countries, Patricia M. Danzon and Jonathan D. Ketcham show that reference pricing approaches may not simply lower prices—they may have effects on the rate of introduction of new drugs, on their success in the market, and therefore on the returns to innovation. Danzon and Ketcham analyze reference pricing in Germany, the Netherlands, and New Zealand. They show that, in countries with the most aggressive reference pricing, the availability of new compounds is significantly delayed. Although their analysis does not address the full welfare consequences of reference pricing and alternative approaches to providing a pharmaceutical benefit, they draw important lessons for the design of a Medicare drug benefit.

Most of those in favor of a Medicare drug benefit share the assumption that any such benefit, at least initially, should be a stand-alone program; that is, it should be complementary to traditional Medicare, not an integrated benefit within Medicare. In this respect, it contrasts with nearly all other health insurance, which includes medication coverage as one of the many categories of covered products and services. The voluntary nature of the Medicare drug benefit and its pricing can make participation unattractive for Medicare beneficiaries who don't expect to spend much money for prescription drugs or otherwise would gain little by participating in the program, giving rise to adverse selection.

According to Mark V. Pauly and Yuhui Zeng, this kind of adverse selection could be a threat to any stand-alone Medicare drug benefit. Examining multiyear data on a large group of workers covered by employment-based health insurance, they find that high-cost users of prescription drugs tend to have high expenditures from one year to the next, so that drug expenditures are more predictable than other health expenditures. This predictability of spending makes a drug benefit particularly vulnerable to adverse selection. Pauly and Zeng show that even large subsidies might fail to keep a voluntary Medicare drug benefit from being subject to a death spiral as the program becomes attractive to an ever-shrinking pool of beneficiaries with ever-increasing average drug expenditures. They also show, however, that bundling the drug benefit with other coverage can mitigate adverse selection.

At the foundation of nearly every Medicare reform proposal is a set of assumptions about the program's future liabilities. Some aspects of these projections, such as the number of Medicare beneficiaries in different age categories, are not controversial, while others, especially per-beneficiary expenditures, are more speculative. Expenditures per beneficiary depend on reimbursement rates, rates of utilization of covered services, and the types and costs of forms of care that are introduced in the coming years. Health status is decisive here; healthier Medicare beneficiaries are expected to use less, and less expensive, health services. High-cost users of Medicare-covered services, especially those who are approaching the end of their lives and those with disabilities, use more.

Recent evidence suggests that rates of disability are declining among the elderly: good news both because it is a harbinger of better quality of life for the elderly and because it suggests that Medicare expenditure growth may well be lower than many had expected. But will the trend continue for future cohorts of the elderly? Jayanta Bhattacharya and colleagues address this question by combining data on current Medicare beneficiaries with data on younger cohorts and projecting future Medicare expenditures based in part on their current health characteristics. They show that declining disability will suppress per-capita Medicare expenditure growth for the near term (less than twenty years), but in subsequent years the rising disability rates among current cohorts of the young will lead to an increase in per-capita Medicare expenditures.

Determining the impact of financial incentives on the quality of care has been a vexing issue for economists and policy makers alike. In their paper, William H. Crown and colleagues develop a novel way to investigate this issue. They examine the effect of out-of-pocket payments for asthma medications on the relative use of controller and reliever medications. Greater use of controllers is a sign of better quality care, and this information allows the authors to learn about the impact of cost sharing on quality. Using data from many large firms, Crown and co-authors find that cost sharing has little impact on the use of controller medications relative to reliever medications. This finding suggests that increases in cost sharing may not be particularly harmful, although it leaves open the question of which policies might be more effective in improving the quality of care.

Beginning in the 1990s, health insurance markets began to change dramatically as several health plans converted from nonprofit to for-profit status, often as a prelude to mergers. This phenomenon was part of the growing consolidation among health plans nationwide. Although considerable public attention has been paid to this phenomenon, and concern about it has increased among employers, hospitals, other health care providers, and the general public, the welfare consequences of such conversions have not been studied thoroughly. Nancy Dean Beaulieu examines a specific for-profit conversion, that of the CareFirst corporation in Maryland, the District of Columbia, and Delaware. Beaulieu reviews the reasons for considering for-profit conversions, the multiple considerations in determining whether a for-profit conversion might be in the public interest, the effects of conversion on the quality of care, and the role of market concentration. She also examines evidence concerning one of the key arguments supporting conversion—that the greater size made possible by the improved access to capital in a conversion would help plans to achieve economies of scale that would otherwise be absent. In addressing these issues, her paper also supplies an agenda for future research on for-profit conversions.

Although the papers included in this volume do not offer policy recommendations, each of them highlights important research findings that bear on current policy initiatives. Each paper is likely to remain relevant to health policy controversies in the years to come.

The conference at which these papers were presented was the work of many people. We are particularly grateful to Donna Mattos and Lita Kimble for arranging the meeting. Funding for the Frontiers in Health Policy Research conference comes from the National Bureau of Economic Research (NBER); we are grateful for their support.

David M. Cutler and Alan M. Garber

1

Reference Pricing of Pharmaceuticals for Medicare: Evidence from Germany, the Netherlands, and New Zealand

Patricia M. Danzon, *University of Pennsylvania, and NBER*
Jonathan D. Ketcham, *University of California, Berkeley, and University of California, San Francisco*

Executive Summary

This paper describes three prototypical systems of therapeutic reference pricing (RP) for pharmaceuticals—Germany, the Netherlands, and New Zealand—and examines their effects on the availability of new drugs, reimbursement levels, manufacturer prices, and out-of-pocket surcharges to patients. RP for pharmaceuticals is not simply analogous to a defined contribution approach to subsidizing insurance coverage. Although a major purpose of RP is to stimulate competition, theory suggests that the achievement of this goal is unlikely, and this is confirmed by the empirical evidence. Other effects of RP differ across countries in predictable ways, reflecting each country's system design and other cost-control policies. New Zealand's RP system has reduced reimbursement and limited the availability of new drugs, particularly more expensive drugs. Compared to these three countries, if RP were applied in the United States, it would likely have a more negative effect on prices of on-patent products because of the more competitive U.S. generic market, and on research and development (R&D) and the future supply of new drugs, because of the much larger U.S. share of global pharmaceutical sales.

I. Introduction

Reference pricing (RP) is an approach to reimbursement for pharmaceuticals that is of considerable policy and research interest. Germany first formally adopted reference pricing in 1989, followed by the Netherlands in 1991 and New Zealand in 1993. British Columbia and Australia adopted reference pricing for specific therapeutic classes in 1995 and 1996, respectively. In the United States, reference pricing has been proposed as a possible approach to drug reimbursement for a comprehensive Medicare drug benefit (Huskamp et al. 2000). Reimbursement based on functional equivalence, which has been suggested for reimbursement of drugs that are already reimbursed under

Medicare Part B, is essentially informal reference pricing. Japan has also debated adopting reference pricing to reform its system of pharmaceutical reimbursement.

Reference pricing is simple in concept: products are classified into clusters based on similar therapeutic effects. The payer sets a reference price (RP) for each cluster based on a relatively low-priced product—for example, the minimum or median price—in the cluster. The RP is the maximum reimbursement for all products in the group. Manufacturers may charge a price above the RP, but in that case the patient must pay the surcharge. If the manufacturer's price is less than the RP, the savings may be shared between the payer and the dispensing pharmacist, depending on system design.

The rationale for RP is to stimulate competition by informing consumers and physicians about substitutability between products. For example, de Vos (1996) explains the objectives of the Dutch reference pricing system:

[C]onsiderable effort was expended by the Dutch government to stimulate price competition in the pharmaceutical market . . . . Only when the necessary information about a specific medicine in relation to its substitutes is readily available can the demand side of the market, i.e., consumers, doctors, patients and insurance companies, make decisions on the fairness of prices. In the Netherlands, this objective was achieved by categorizing medicines into groups of interchangeable drugs and making doctors and patients aware of the interchangeability of medicines within such groups. (de Vos, 1996)

Because reference pricing controls the reimbursement but not the manufacturer's price, this approach is usually viewed as less restrictive than price controls and has been adopted in countries that previously had free pricing. Reference pricing is also in some ways similar to a defined contribution approach to insurance subsidization. The effects could be quite different, however, when applied to pharmaceuticals, as we discuss below.

In analyzing RP programs, it is critical to distinguish between generic referencing, which applies only to generically equivalent products with the same active ingredient and formulation, and therapeutic RP programs, which extend referencing to products with different active ingredients. Generic referencing is a well-established practice in the United States through maximum allowable charge (MAC) programs that are used by Medicaid and by some managed-care programs to reimburse for multisource compounds, that is, off-patent compounds with at least one generic product. The payer typically defines the MAC as the maximum reimbursement for all products with a given molecule, formulation, and strength, based on the price of a relatively cheap generic. A patient who wants the originator brand must pay any excess of the brand price over the MAC. Thus, U.S. MAC programs are reference pricing in all but name, and similar generic referencing systems have existed in the United Kingdom and some Canadian provinces for many years. Such generic referencing is relatively noncontroversial. It conserves third-party funds without exposing patients to significant risk because it applies substitution only between generically equivalent products that have demonstrated bioequivalence to the originator product. Moreover, because generic referencing applies only to off-patent products, it does not reduce effective patent life for originator products and hence has minimal effect on incentives for research and development (R&D). Since the 1990s, generic referencing has been adopted by a growing number of countries, including Sweden, Italy, Spain, and Denmark.

Therapeutic referencing, as developed by Germany, the Netherlands, and New Zealand, extends the concept of substitutability from generically equivalent products (same molecule) to different molecules for the same indication. Therapeutic referencing is far more controversial because it treats compounds with different active ingredients as equivalent, despite possible differences in efficacy and/or side effects for at least some patients. Patients for whom the reference-priced product does not work face either higher copayments or health risks if they switch, which may be nonoptimal insurance coverage. Moreover, by clustering on-patent compounds with off-patent compounds, RP may reduce effective patent life and significantly affect incentives for R&D.

A full analysis of reference pricing would address its effects on patients, on manufacturers, and on the efficiency of resource use. These issues are discussed below, but the empirical analysis is necessarily more limited, as is the existing literature. Previous studies have described the design of various countries' RP systems and reported data on drug spending either in aggregate or for a limited number of products in individual countries (see, for example, Danzon 2001, Lopez-Casasnovas and Puig-Junoy 2001, Jonsson 2001, and Ioannides-Demos et al. 2002). Few studies of reference pricing use micro data. Studies of RP in Germany concluded that brand manufacturers generally dropped their prices to the reference price (Remit Consultants 1991, Maasen 1995, Danzon and Liu 1996). Similarly, Pavcnik (2002) found that manufacturers of hypoglycemics and H2-antagonists reduced their prices in response to the introduction of RP in Germany, and that branded products were affected more than generics. In other circumstances, however patients have faced significant surcharges and have switched away from surcharged drugs. Following the implementation of RP in British Columbia, patients reduced their utilization of higher-priced ACE inhibitors in favor of other antihypertensives with lower out-of-pocket costs (Schneeweiss et al. 2002). Thomas, Mann, and Williams (1998) report that in New Zealand, following a tender for the hydroxyl-methylglutaryl coenzyme A (HMGCoA) reductase inhibitor class, fluvastatin tendered the lowest price and established the subsidy (RP) for the class. Patients receiving simvastatin faced a surcharge of NZ$50.63 per month. Patients who switched to the fully subsidized fluvastatin experienced a significant increase in total cholesterol, LDL cholesterol, and triglyceride levels ($p < 0.01$).

Some of these results might suggest that RP succeeds in its objective of encouraging competition. The evidence from Germany is not representative of comprehensive RP systems, however, because new on-patent products were exempt from RP after 1996. Estimation of the effects of RP alone are confounded in all countries because other cost-control measures were adopted. For example, in 1993, Germany introduced a global drug budget with physicians at risk for spending overruns, which strongly influenced physician prescribing (see Ulrich and Wille 1996), and in 1996, the Netherlands superimposed strict price controls on reference pricing. Because each country's RP system is different, generalization from single-country studies may be inappropriate. None of these previous studies has compared the effects of RP across countries with different system designs, and none has examined the effects of RP on the availability of drugs.

In this paper we first describe the main features of the RP systems in Germany, the Netherlands, and New Zealand and each country's other cost-control policies that may confound estimation of the effects of RP. Section III outlines a model of manufacturer response to reference pricing and develops hypotheses about the effects of RP on price competition and the availability of new drugs. Our empirical analysis combines data on reference prices from government sources and data on manufacturer prices from the market research firm IMS Health for five major therapeutic categories in 1998.[1] Section IV describes the data. Section V reports the evidence on the availability of new products and the effects of competition and other factors on RPs, manufacturer prices, and patient surcharges. Section VI summarizes these findings from the three countries. Section VII compares RP to other possible models of insurance benefit design, in particular, a percentage co-insurance rate and tiered formularies. Section VIII discusses the implications of these findings for the proposed use of RP in the United States. The appendix summarizes differences among RP, price controls, and tiered formularies.

We find that RP has significantly reduced the availability of new compounds in New Zealand, which has the most aggressive RP system, and this effect is greatest for high-priced new products. There is no evidence that RP has encouraged competition, which is consistent with the hypothesis that prices tend to converge to and remain at the RP in the absence of other interventions. The findings that RP has tended to reduce reimbursement for recently launched products and that originator products are more likely to charge surcharges suggest that RP may reduce manufacturer incentives for innovation.

The experience of RP in these three countries has lessons for the United States and for other countries that may consider it. But we conclude that if RP were adopted in the United States, for example, for a Medicare drug benefit, it could have a much more negative effect on prices of on-patent drugs and on incentives for R&D than occurred in these three countries. The structure of retail pharmacy in the United States results in a more price-competitive generic market, which in turn would put greater pressure on on-patent drug prices than occurs in other countries. Significant reductions in on-patent revenues in the United States could have a significant effect on incentives to develop new drugs given the dominant U.S. share of global pharmaceutical sales. Thus, whereas the United States is less likely than these smaller markets to experience nonlaunch of new drugs that are already advanced in the pipeline, the long-term effects on the supply of new drugs are likely to be more severe if RP is applied in the United States.

Reference pricing as analyzed here, which sets a single reimbursement price for different products that are considered interchangeable in a given country, should not be confused with cross national referencing, which is a form of price regulation used by many countries. Cross-national referencing sets the price of each product to the mean or median price of that same product in other countries. Such cross-national referencing is not expected to encourage price competition between therapeutic substitutes; rather, it constrains a manufacturer's ability to price-discriminate across countries for a given product, and the manufacturer's price cannot exceed the regulated price.

Reference pricing is also distinct from tiered formularies used by pharmacy benefit managers (PBMs) in the United States. In a tiered formulary, products considered more cost-effective are placed on the preferred tier and carry a lower copayment than nonpreferred products on the higher tier. For example, the copayment structure may be $5, $15, and $30 for a generic, preferred brand, and nonpreferred brand, respectively. The PBM negotiates discounts from drug manufacturers in return for preferred formulary status and the implied increase in market share. Thus, tiered formularies are used to promote price competition actively among therapeutic substitute drugs. However, PBMs usually apply RP only to generically equivalent, multisource compounds; that is, the preferred product in a molecule is a generic and patients who want the higher-priced originator brand must pay the excess of the brand price over the generic price. For therapeutic substitutes, although lower-priced products are more likely to be preferred, a product that is priced higher but is more effective may be on the preferred tier and reimbursed at a higher price than a less effective compound on either the same or the nonpreferred tier. Thus, compared to RP, tiered formularies are designed to stimulate competition through negotiated discounts in return for preferred formulary status, and tiered formularies are more flexible in paying higher reimbursement for products that offer better efficacy, fewer side effects, or in other ways are more cost-effective. Implications of these differences between RP and tiered formularies are discussed in Section VIII.

II.   Reference Pricing in Germany, the Netherlands, and New Zealand

Every RP system must define the rules for clustering drugs, including classifying new products, and for setting reference prices. This section describes the main features of each country's RP system through 1998, the year of our data. Post-1998 changes are also mentioned when they are relevant to understanding the evolution of these systems. We also describe each country's other pharmaceutical cost-control policies that potentially influence drug prices and volumes and hence must be considered in interpreting results.[2]

Germany
Germany adopted reference pricing in 1989. The federal government defined broad parameters but implementation was left largely to the

Association of Sickness Funds (Bundesverband der Betriebskrankenkassen [BKK]). The BKK defined the clustering system for drugs, subject to the approval of the physicians' association. The BKK also determined the reference prices.[3]

Classification. Unlike the Netherlands and New Zealand, Germany's RP system was phased in for different types of products and was not intended to be fully comprehensive. Class 1 includes products with the same active ingredient (generic referencing); class 2 applies to therapeutically and pharmacologically similar active ingredients; and class 3 applies to compounds with comparable therapeutic effect, especially combinations. Litigation over the definition of groups for classes 2 and 3 (particularly the clustering of newer, patented products with off-patent products) slowed implementation.

New Products. Following legislation in 1996, new on-patent products have been exempt from RP and are reimbursed in full without price controls. New generic products can join existing clusters with reimbursement at the prevailing RP.

As of January 2000, reference prices covered 197 active ingredients in class 1, 166 active ingredients in twenty-three groups in class 2, and thirty-one combinations in class 3. These drugs accounted for roughly 50.3 percent of expenditures and 64 percent of scripts under Germany's statutory health system (VFA 2000).

Setting the Reference Price. Germany's method for setting RP levels was designed to reflect market prices more closely than in other countries. For each group, a standard formulation (for example, regular tablets of 20 mg strength) was selected and an RP was set for that formulation within the range of manufacturer prices, with a higher RP set for product classes with few generic suppliers to encourage entry. The relative RPs for different formulations, strengths, and pack sizes were based on a quasi-hedonic regression (of Cobb-Douglas form) applied to manufacturer prices. RPs are revised annually, based on a review of actual manufacturer prices. In Germany, manufacturers have sometimes priced below the RP, which leads to reductions in RP levels in classes where the prevailing RP exceeded the average manufacturer price. As discussed below, this tendency for manufacturers to price below the RP in

Germany probably reflects incentives created by the physician drug budgets rather than the RP system.

Physician, Pharmacy, and Patient Incentives. Physicians who prescribe a product priced above the RP are legally required to explain to the patient why the surcharged product is necessary. This stipulation creates an incentive for physicians to avoid products priced above the RP, assuming that an explanation requires physician time that is not reimbursed. Information on product prices is made available to physicians.

Retail pharmacy in Germany is strictly regulated with respect to pricing, margins and entry. German pharmacists have traditionally lacked the authorization and the incentive to substitute low-priced generics or parallel imports (PIs) for higher-priced originator products. Until 2001, pharmacists were permitted to substitute a generic for a brand only if the physician prescribed generically, which occurred in only 5 percent of scripts (Schoffski 1996).[4] German pharmacy dispensing margins are regulated and yield a higher absolute margin on higher-priced drugs, despite a declining percentage. To counteract these perverse incentives, Germany enacted legislation in 2001 that requires pharmacists to substitute a cheaper parallel import or generic if either is available.

Other Cost Controls: Physician Drug Budgets. The adoption of RP in 1989 did not stop the growth of drug spending. This outcome was hardly surprising because Germany's RP system applied initially to multisource products primarily. Of these, generics already accounted for 53 percent of scripts (Ulrich and Wille 1996). Moreover RP does not constrain volume or shifting to higher-priced products in other groups.[5] Faced with the cost pressures of reunification with the former East Germany, in 1993 Germany increased patient copayments; imposed a 5 percent price cut on non-RP drugs; and adopted a national drug budget that set a limit on outpatient drug expenditures, initially at the 1991 spending level and subsequently updated by the GDP growth rate, with physicians collectively at risk for the first DM280m of any drug budget overrun (and the pharmaceutical industry at risk for the next DM280m). These measures led to a 19 percent decline in pharmaceutical expenditures; a decline in the number of prescriptions; and switching to cheaper products, including generics (Ulrich and Wille 1996). Some regions implemented physician-specific prescribing protocols and drug budgets, based on medical specialty and patient mix, but implementation was slow. The national drug budget was abolished in 2002.

Summarizing, under the German RP system without the drug budget, physicians, pharmacists, and patients did not have strong financial incentives to prefer drugs priced below the RP; hence, manufacturers had little incentive to set prices below the RP.[6] To the extent that dynamic price competition with pricing below the RP occurred in Germany, this must be attributed to physicians being at risk for drug budget overruns, not to reference pricing.

The Netherlands

In the 1980s, relatively high prices and rapid pharmaceutical spending growth in the Netherlands made drugs a target for cost control, despite relatively low drug spending compared to other European countries. In 1991, a reference price system was introduced with the objective of improving information, cost-consciousness, and price competition (de Vos 1996).

Classification. Unlike Germany, the Dutch RP system was comprehensive from the outset; that is, it included almost all on-patent and off-patent drugs. Clusters were defined based initially on five criteria, which were reduced to four; then in 1999, they were reduced to the single criterion of clinically relevant differences in effects that are decisive for prescribing choices of doctors.[7] Classification decisions are made by the Ministry of Health, with input from a panel of medical advisers. The clustering of new products has been frequently litigated, which has led to some revisions of the clusters over time. For example, the grouping of the new, more expensive migraine therapy sumatriptan in the same category with two older ergotamine products was challenged and settled only after a five-year lawsuit (Merck Frosst Canada 1996).

New Products. The Netherlands originally placed new, nonclusterable products on a separate list, list 1b, to be reimbursed in full. Following rapid growth of spending on list 1b products (over 20 percent annually), list 1b was closed in July 1993. New products could be reimbursed only if they joined an existing cluster, unless they were indicated for a disease for which no treatment existed. This stipulation led to a growing list of "waiting-room" products that were not admitted to outpatient reimbursement, even though they had marketing approval and might be available to hospital inpatients. Some manufacturers accepted listing with existing groups as the only way to get new products reimbursed; for example, the selective norepinephrine reuptake inhibitors (SNRIs) were grouped with selective serotonin reuptake inhibitors (SSRIs) and angiotensin-II antagonists with ACE inhibitors.

Since 1997, a new product that is not clusterable may be reimbursed if it is indicated for a disease for which no pharmacotherapeutic treatment is available; if another treatment exists, the new drug may be reimbursed only if it is cost-effective relative to the alternative and if sufficient budget funds are available.

Setting the Reference Price. The Netherlands' approach to the problem of defining a common price for different compounds is to define a standard daily dose for each compound, based on the World Health Organization (WHO) defined daily dose (DDD) system. The average price per DDD for each molecule is calculated as the unweighted average of the price per DDD of all originator and generic products in the molecule. The RP is then set at the median of the distribution, across molecules, of 1990 prices. These 1991 RPs remained in effect until 1999 apparently because this RP system created no incentive for manufacturers to reduce list prices below the RP and because list prices that were initially below the RP reportedly converged on the RP. The government therefore added direct price controls, as described below.

Pharmacy Reimbursement and Incentives. As in Germany, retail pharmacy in the Netherlands is regulated with respect to entry and pricing. Pharmacists are authorized to substitute a generic or a PI provided that the script is generically written and the patient is informed.[8] Pharmacists receive a fixed dispensing fee per script, rather than a percentage of the product price, to encourage substitution toward cheaper products. To encourage dispensing of generics and PIs further, the pharmacist can retain one-third of the difference between the reimbursement price or RP and the list price of the cheaper substitute. However, pharmacists capture 100 percent of any manufacturer discounts below the list price, whereas they receive only one-third of any differential between the list price and the RP. Manufacturers therefore compete for market share by offering discounts off the list price rather than by reducing the list price. The magnitude of these discounts was estimated at NG300 to 400 million in 1994 (de Vos 1996). Thus, price competition occurred in the Netherlands but not because of the RP system. And it was not in a form that reduced list prices to generate savings for payers. In July 1998, the government introduced a partial "clawback" of the discounts through a 4.7 percent reduction in reimbursement rates to pharmacies.

Other Cost Controls: Maximum Price Regulation. After a 5 percent price cut in 1994, the Netherlands superimposed a new system (the Maximum of Price Law) of maximum price regulation in 1996 to reduce prices below levels generated by the RP system. The maximum price for each molecule/dosage form/strength was hereafter based on the average price in Belgium, France, Germany, and the United Kingdom, including generics and originator products.[9] This change imposed a 15 percent price reduction on average and capped prices for many products below their RP. Thus, in the Netherlands, the Maximum Price Law made RPs nonbinding for many products and introduced dispersion of prices of different compounds within an RP cluster because of the variation in their maximum prices. In 1999, the RP levels were reduced based on these regulated maximum prices.

Thus, although reference pricing in the Netherlands was intended to promote price competition, in practice most list prices, including generics, reportedly clustered close to the RP until the Maximum Price Law invoked foreign price levels to force prices below the RPs. Competition did thrive but in the form of discounts off list prices rather than lower list prices, leading to profit for pharmacists, not savings for the government, at least initially. This competition was driven by the pharmacists' authorization and incentives to substitute generically equivalent products, including parallel imports, and was quite independent of therapeutic reference pricing.

New Zealand

New Zealand's outpatient pharmaceutical expenditures are managed by the Pharmaceutical Management Agency (Pharmac), a not-for-profit company owned by the Health Financing Authority. Pharmac's functions are similar to those of competing pharmacy benefit managers (PBMs) in the United States, except that Pharmac has monopsony power. Pharmac defines the Pharmaceutical Schedule, a formulary or positive list of roughly 3,000 prescription drugs and related products that are eligible for subsidy (reimbursement); negotiates prices with manufacturers and sets subsidy levels, if any; and designs and operates other cost-control strategies. The Schedule lists the price of each drug, the subsidy level, and the guidelines or conditions under which the drug may be prescribed. Consumers may purchase other approved drugs but without public subsidy. Pharmac is advised by a Pharmacology and Therapeutics Advisory Committee (PTAC) comprised of medical specialists and general practitioners whose role is to provide independent advice on the pharmacological and therapeutic consequences of proposed amendments to the Pharmaceutical Schedule, including review of company applications for Schedule listing and requests by Pharmac for removing items from the reimbursement list. Reference pricing was introduced in July 1993 with the intent to "reduce the excessive market segmentation based on brand marketing, which previously allowed suppliers to establish markets that were free from price competition" (Kletchko, Moore, and Jones 1995).

Classification.   Almost all prescription drugs that are reimbursed in New Zealand are subject to reference pricing. Therapeutic subgroups are relatively broadly defined as "pharmaceuticals that produce the same or similar therapeutic effects in treating the same or similar conditions" (Kletchko, Moore, and Jones 1995). Patent status is not considered.

New Products.   New products are generally reimbursed only if they join an existing subgroup, which requires offering a price below the prevailing RP (see below). A new product that is not clusterable into an existing subgroup may sometimes be reimbursed if Pharmac and the manufacturer can agree on a reimbursement price. For example, Serevent was listed after five years of negotiations; Imigran tablets were submitted for review four times in five years (Merck Frosst Canada 1996).

Setting the Reference Price.   New Zealand sets the RP at the lowest price in each subgroup, regardless of patent status. In principle, manufacturers may charge a price above the RP. However, Pharmac may eliminate all subsidy for a product if a substitute product is available at a lower price and if Pharmac considers that the higher-priced product has no additional clinical benefit.

Unlike Germany and the Netherlands, Pharmac has used its monopsony power and the RP system to negotiate price cuts on new products, which then apply to all existing products in the RP cluster. Specifically, a new product is admitted to reimbursement in an existing RP cluster only if it is priced significantly below the prevailing RP. For generics, the first generic must offer a 30 percent price cut relative to the brand, the second must offer an additional 20 percent cut, and so on, although the required discounts for generics are becoming less rigid. These lower prices then define the new, lower RP for all products in that subgroup. Tendering is also used, with the lowest tendered price becoming the subsidy level for all drugs in the group.

Alternatively, the manufacturer of a new product may also offer a cross-therapeutic deal by reducing its price on another of its products in another therapeutic subgroup. A manufacturer may rationally prefer to give a large price cut on an old product with a small market share rather than accept a low launch price on a new product that it hopes will gain significant volume. Thus, Pharmac uses cross-therapeutic deals to negotiate larger price cuts than manufacturers might be willing to offer on new products. For example, in 1996, a 40 percent price cut on Tagamet was offered in return for a listing on the Schedule for Famvir, thereby reducing the RP of all H2 antagonists by 40 percent (Pharma Pricing Review 1996). The Schedule is updated monthly. Reference prices may thus change whenever a new product enters the market or following a therapeutic group review initiated by Pharmac.

Physician, Patient, and Pharmacist Incentives. Physicians and patients in New Zealand traditionally have had little incentive to be price-conscious. The patient copayment is the lesser of the cost of the drug or a fixed payment (which depends on welfare status) per script, plus any surcharge over the RP if the manufacturer's price exceeds the subsidy. Nonfinancial strategies to influence physician prescribing include provision of information, limiting certain drugs to specialists and/or specific conditions, and counterdetailing. Some physician associations also provide voluntary guidelines to their members, monthly charting of prescribing relative to the average, and similar services.

Retail pharmacy in New Zealand is heavily regulated. As in Germany and the Netherlands, restrictions on entry, prohibitions on nonpharmacist ownership and on branching, and other measures discourage retail price competition on drugs. Pharmacists were paid a fixed dispensing fee per script plus a percentage of the price. Although generic substitution rules permit the pharmacist to substitute generics unless the physician explicitly prescribes the brand and writes "no substitution," the traditional percentage margin reimbursement undermined incentives to substitute cheaper products that would yield a lower margin. In 1998, the government proposed replacing this fee based on percentage-of-price with a fixed dispensing fee.

Other Cost-Control Policies.   In addition to RP for controlling prices, Pharmac uses other strategies to control drug volume and expenditures. National guidelines limit the prescribing of expensive medicines to certain conditions and/or to specialists. For example, Prozac was initially restricted and then made subject to an annual budget cap. In pay-to-play contracts, suppliers are paid a negotiated, up-front amount to make a product available at a lower price. Tendering, sole supply, and preferred supplier contracts are used to offer a supplier a larger market share in return for a lower price. In price-volume contracts, the price varies inversely with volume. Many generics are subject to such contracts. In average daily dose contracts, the subsidy is tied to a specified average daily dose and the supplier must pay a rebate if this average dose is exceeded, thereby shifting the risk of increasing daily dosage strength to the supplier. Listing of a new drug may also be contingent on the manufacturer accepting risk sharing through a capped annual budget with paybacks for overruns and possibly price reductions on drugs already listed.

In summary, although New Zealand's RP system by itself does not encourage competition, Pharmac has negotiated price cuts as a condition of admitting new products to reimbursement through the RP system, in addition to several other bargaining strategies.

III.   Modeling Effects of Reference Pricing

A complete analysis of the effects of reference pricing would consider its effects on patients, including availability of drugs, out-of-pocket payments, and health outcomes; effects on drug expenditures and any increase in physician or hospital visits to deal with complications or prescription changes; and effects on manufacturers, including prices and volumes of new drugs and hence incentives for innovation.[10]

In this paper, we analyze the effects of RP on product launch decisions and hence the availability of new products and its effects on the reimbursement (RP level), manufacturer price, and implied patient surcharge, conditional on launch. Volume responses to surcharges and other factors are described in Danzon and Ketcham (2004, forthcoming). Our data set provides six months of data on RP levels and drug sales in our three countries in 1998. The great majority of products in our sample are under RP—96 percent in the Netherlands, 92 percent in New Zealand, and 62 percent in Germany, where on-patent products launched after 1996 and older products with few competitors were exempt from RP. The almost universal coverage of RP in the Netherlands and New Zealand, and the fact that we have only six months of sales data, preclude the use of formal difference-in-differences analysis to estimate the effects of RP. Our empirical analysis exploits the difference between drug cohorts by year of launch and exploits the differences among the three countries in their RP systems and other cost-control strategies. The following section outlines specific predictions.

Effects of RP on the Launch of New Compounds

Even in the absence of RP, other factors may lead to differences among the three countries in the launch of new compounds. If each country were a separate pharmaceutical market (so that manufacturers could pursue country-specific pricing policies), more products would be launched in markets with larger potential sales, assuming that any product launch entails certain fixed administrative and regulatory costs, independent of its potential sales. Thus, based on population size alone, Germany is expected to attract the most new compounds, followed by the Netherlands and then New Zealand.

In practice, although pharmaceutical price regulation remains a national prerogative, price spillovers across markets are potentially significant due to parallel trade and regulation based on foreign prices, so that a low price charged in one country can undercut prices in potentially higher-price markets. Parallel trade is authorized between member states of the European Union (EU).[11] Regulation based on foreign prices occurs formally and informally in many countries. This potential for cross-national price spillovers is expected to make manufacturers less willing to launch new compounds in countries with low prices, especially countries with small potential sales volume (for evidence, see Danzon, Wang, and Wang 2002).

The reference price systems in our three countries are expected to exacerbate their relative attractiveness as markets for new compounds based solely on market size. Germany's RP system created negligible, if any, disincentive to the launch of new compounds because Germany defined clusters relatively narrowly and new patented products were exempt from RP after 1996. New Zealand's RP system is expected to have the most negative effect on the launch of new compounds, particularly potentially high-priced compounds, because New Zealand has the broadest criteria for defining product clusters and usually requires the manufacturer of a new product to offer a price below the established RP as a condition of being reimbursed in that cluster (or give a price cut in another cluster). Although the Netherlands, like New Zealand, required that most new products join an existing RP cluster as a condition of reimbursement, the Dutch criteria for product clusters were less broad than those in New Zealand, and RP levels were set relatively high (at the median of 1991 prices, which were reportedly high relative to European average prices, with no revision until 1999). After 1996, the Netherlands' prices were capped at the median of prices in the United Kingdom, Germany, France, and Belgium. Thus, it is an empirical question whether the resulting prices were sufficiently low to discourage the launch of new compounds.[12] In 1998, the availability of new compounds in the Netherlands is expected to be similar to that observed in Germany, assuming that Dutch prices were constrained to levels similar to those in Germany and the United Kingdom, and that early delays in admitting new products to the Dutch RP system had been resolved.

Effects of RP on Drug Prices
If each country were a separate market, a drug manufacturer's pricing response to RP would depend on how RP and any other cost-control policies affect the price elasticity of demand, which in turn depends on the incentives of physicians; patients; and, if substitution is permitted, pharmacists. Under RP, patient demand is expected to be elastic at prices above the RP unless patients are informed about any differential product characteristics. Physician demand is also expected to be relatively elastic at prices above the RP, both as good agents for patients and because physicians may incur an unreimbursed time cost if they prescribe a drug that is priced above the RP. Physician drug budgets are expected to increase physician price sensitivity, including sensitivity to prices below the RP. Pharmacists are expected to be highly price sensitive if they can profit from the margin between the RP reimbursement and their actual acquisition cost of a generic substitute or parallel import. However, the effects of RP in a specific country may be mitigated by concern for cross-market spillover effects to prices in other countries. We discuss how these considerations apply in each of our three countries.

In Germany, because RP applies only to therapeutic categories with multiple close substitute products, a monopolistic competition model is appropriate.[13] Assuming monopolistic competition, the manufacturer's demand curve becomes kinked at the RP. At prices above the RP, demand is relatively elastic because patients must pay for any surcharge and physicians face a time cost of explaining to patients if they prescribe a surcharged product. The kinked demand model predicts that manufacturers of originator and other relatively high-priced products would drop their prices to the RP unless this within-country elasticity effect is mitigated by potential revenue loss through cross-market spillovers—for example, if reducing the price in Germany would result in lower prices in other countries, say, Italy or the Netherlands, which both cross-reference Germany in setting their own prices.[14]

Germany's RP system alone created no incentives for physicians, patients, or pharmacists to be price-sensitive at prices below the RP; hence, the RP system created no incentives for dynamic competition to reduce prices over time. Because Germany's physicians were financially at risk for drug budget overruns, however, their general price sensitivity due to drug budgets could in theory create incentives for manufacturers to charge prices below the RP. Such competitive pressure on prices is expected to be greater in classes with multiple generic substitutes (same compound and hence, almost perfect substitutes) than from therapeutic substitutes (different compounds and hence, imperfect substitutes). Thus, in Germany, prices are predicted to be inversely related to the number of competitors, particularly generic competitors, in a class. Because Germany revised the RP levels periodically based on actual manufacturer prices, RP levels are also predicted to be inversely related to the number of competitor products in a class. But note that, aside from the initial incentive for high-priced products to drop their price to the RP, these dynamic competitive effects in Germany result from the physician drug budgets, not from the structure of the RP system.

In the Netherlands, predicting the effects of the RP system is complicated by the maximum price ceilings. Under the RP system alone, the kinked demand model predicts that in classes with multiple competing products, prices would converge to the RP, except that surcharges may survive for originator products if concerns about external price spillovers dominate market share concerns in the Netherlands. Manufacturers had no incentive to cut list prices below the RP because neither physicians nor patients had incentives to be price-sensitive below the RP and pharmacists were more price-sensitive to discounts off the list price than to reductions in list prices. Moreover discounts would not trigger price spillovers to other countries. (Note that discounts off list prices are unobservable in our data, which include only list prices.) For product classes with few competitors, oligopoly may be a more appropriate assumption; although many models are possible, aggressive price competition is unlikely. Thus, under assumptions of either monopolistic competition or oligopoly, RP alone would not induce competition.

The Netherlands' experience with RP was dominated, however, by the 1996 Maximum Price Law, which imposed binding, molecule-specific price ceilings that were frequently below the RP for each compound. There was no incentive for manufacturers to set list prices below these price ceilings. Thus, in the Netherlands, neither prices nor RPs are expected to be influenced by competition induced by the RP system. The 1998 RPs reflect the price distribution that prevailed in 1991, when the RP system was enacted. The 1998 prices reflect the regulated price caps based on foreign prices, which may imply some price dispersion depending on prices in the benchmark countries. Consequently, prices in the Netherlands are expected to vary inversely with the number of competitors to the extent that such conditions prevailed in the benchmark foreign countries (United Kingdom, Germany, Belgium, and France). In fact, market and regulatory systems in all these countries would plausibly lead to an inverse relation between prices and the number of competitor products (see Danzon and Chao 2000); in which case, prices in the Netherlands should vary inversely with the number of competitor products. However, this would reflect foreign experience and assumes correlation across countries in the number of competitors by therapeutic class.

In New Zealand, the kinked demand model predicts that manufacturer prices would converge down to the RP, in the absence of manufacturer concerns about cross-market spillovers and assuming elastic demand at prices above the RP. Although neither physicians, patients pharmacists have incentives to be price-sensitive at prices below the RP, RP levels and prices are nevertheless predicted to be inversely related to the number of competitors in a class because Pharmac uses its monopsony power to negotiate a reduction in the RP as a condition of permitting a new product to join an existing class.

In summary, the structural differences among the three countries' RP systems, together with differences in other controls, lead to the specific predictions discussed in the subsections below.

Availability of New Compounds. The probability of the launch of new compounds is expected to be greatest in Germany and least in New Zealand, particularly for new compounds launched after 1993 and for relatively high-priced products.

Price Compression. Reference pricing is expected to compress the range of reimbursement levels (subsidies) and manufacturer prices within each therapeutic class, with greater compression in countries with broad criteria for defining classes and where the RP is based on the minimum manufacturer price in the class. Greatest downward compression of RP levels is therefore expected in New Zealand, which has the broadest criteria for defining clusters and sets the RP at the lowest manufacturer price in each cluster. Germany's RP system is expected to impose the least compression on both RPs and manufacturer prices; however, Germany's physician drug budgets create additional incentives for manufacturers to constrain relatively high prices and even price below the RP, which confounds the predictions based on RP alone. The Dutch RP system alone created incentives for convergence of list prices to the RP, but the 1996 Maximum Price Law capped many prices below their RPs and led to the dispersion of prices below the RP. Thus, for the Netherlands, price dispersion within classes is possible due to price regulation, not to competition induced by the RP system.[15]

Originators Versus Generics. Reference pricing is expected to reduce RP (subsidy) levels and manufacturers' prices of originator products relative to subsidies and prices of parallel imports and generic substitutes because RP levels are generally based on relatively low-priced products in each class without regard to patent status. Prices of originators may still be higher, but the difference is expected to be smaller under RP than under free pricing. Unfortunately, none of our countries provides a benchmark for completely unregulated pricing. For some analysis, we use Germany as a benchmark of relatively free pricing of new products because it exempted new patented products from its RP system after 1996.

Price Competition.   Although RP was intended to stimulate competition, this effect is limited to an incentive for high-priced products (usually originators) in crowded categories to drop prices to the RP. There is no incentive for manufacturers to price below the RP and indeed, if RPs were set above the lowest price, these prices may converge upward. Thus, RP alone creates no incentive for dynamic price competition in the absence of other controls or structural features that make physicians, patients, or pharmacists sensitive to prices below the RP. In Germany, however, drug budgets created incentives for manufacturers to compete on price, and in New Zealand, Pharmac used its monopsony power to bargain for a price reduction as a condition of admitting new products to reimbursement in an established class. Thus, in both Germany and New Zealand, prices and RPs are predicted to vary inversely with the number of competitors. For the Netherlands, any apparent influence of the number of competitors on RPs reflects competitive pressures as of 1991, before the introduction of the RP system; for prices, any influence of the number of competitors reflects competition or regulation in the benchmark countries from which the price caps were imported.

Surcharges.   The kinked demand model predicts that demand would be highly elastic at prices above the RP and that manufacturers would drop prices to the RP (zero surcharge) if products in a class are good substitutes or if patients are unaware of any differences in efficacy or side effects possibly because physicians do not take the time to explain. Thus, surcharges are expected only for products with relatively inelastic demand because of actual or perceived superior characteristics, or if cross-national spillovers risks are significant. Both effects are more likely for originator products than for generics.

IV.   Data

The data for this study include, for each country, all products with sales reported by IMS in the first half of 1998, for five major therapeutic categories: anti-ulcerants (A02); hypoglycemics (A10); antihyperlipidemics (C10); antidepressants (N06); and antihypertensives, which are further subdivided by mode of action into cardiac therapy (C01), diuretics (C03), beta blockers (C07), calcium channel blockers (C08), and ACE inhibitors and angiotensin-II antagonists (C09).[16] We obtained sales data from IMS and RP (subsidy) data from the agency responsible for reimbursement in each country.

We use the IMS data to calculate price per dose (IMS standard unit) at manufacturer prices in U.S. dollars.[17] The data from these two sources were matched at the pack level to permit comparisons of prices to subsidy levels. A surcharge per standard unit for each pack was defined as the price minus the subsidy per standard unit. Extreme values of this surcharge were used to remove outlier packs. Molecule-level prices, RPs, and surcharges are defined as volume-weighted averages of the corresponding pack-level variables for each country.

We define two measures of age for each molecule. Country-specific age is measured in months from the first launch date of any product in the molecule in a given country to the latest date of the observation period (June 1998). Global molecule age is the maximum of the three country-specific age variables. These age measures apply to all products in a given molecule. Other measures of product value and market competition are defined below. Measures of molecule age and the number of generic and therapeutic competitors were calculated before the removal of outlier packs.

V. Empirical Results

Availability of New Compounds

Of the 200 molecules in our sample, Germany has 175, of which 109 (62 percent) are reference-priced; the Netherlands has 118, of which 108 (92 percent) are reference-priced; and New Zealand has 95, of which 91 (96 percent) are reference-priced. The much larger number of molecules available in Germany is consistent with expectations given Germany's larger market size and its relatively narrow criteria for defining RP clusters, flexibility in setting RP levels, and exemption from RP of on-patent products launched after 1996. Similarly, New Zealand's relatively small number of launches is consistent with predictions given its small population and its comprehensive RP system, with relatively broad clusters and requirements for price cuts from new entrants.

Table 1.1 lists the availability of molecules categorized by their global molecule age (first launch date in our three countries) to test whether New Zealand and, to a lesser extent, the Netherlands experienced reduced availability after 1991, compared to Germany, because of their more restrictive RP systems. This rough difference-in-differences analysis uses Germany as the control group because Germany's RP

Table 1.1
Availability of molecules, as of 1998 by molecule global launch date

Global launch	Total	Germany	The Netherlands	New Zealand
Prior to 1987	126	114	69	67
		90%	55%	53%
1987–1990	27	24	21	15
		89%	78%	56%
1991–1994	22	20	13	10
		91%	59%	45%
After 1994	25	17	15	3
		68%	60%	12%

was least restrictive and new on-patent compounds were exempt after 1996. More recent drug cohorts are expected to be less widely available in all three countries because of lags in diffusion.

For Germany, the percentage of molecules available does not show a strong trend after the introduction of reference pricing in 1989 compared to the pre-RP period, with roughly 90 percent of compounds launched. After 1994, this declines to 68 percent of the post-1994 cohort launched, which may reflect diffusion lags with censored data. The Netherlands has fewer molecules launched after the introduction of reference pricing in 1991 (59 to 60 percent) compared to 78 percent in 1987 to 1990 immediately prior to RP. This finding suggests that the Netherlands' requirement that most new products join established RP clusters as a condition of reimbursement deterred the launch of some new compounds. This conclusion is tentative because the Netherlands also has relatively few (55 percent) of the pre-1987 cohort. RP may have led to early withdrawal of some older molecules in the Netherlands because of relatively low reimbursement (see figure 1.1), so our data would underestimate the total number of older (pre-1987) molecules launched. Withdrawing cheap old products that might reduce the RP for new products could be a rational strategy for manufacturers, particularly in classes with few competitors.

For New Zealand, there is a dramatic decline in availability for more recent molecule cohorts. Whereas New Zealand has 53 percent of molecules launched before 1987, it has 45 percent of molecules launched from 1991 to 1994 and only 12 percent of molecules launched from 1995 to 1998. This very low availability of the 1990s cohort of new molecules in New Zealand cannot simply be attributed to its generally longer launch lags.[18] The sharply reduced availability of new compounds

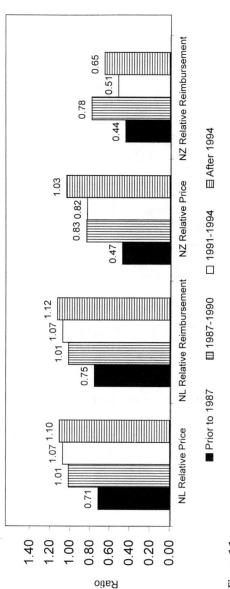

Figure 1.1
NL and NZ molecule prices and reimbursements relative to German price by country launch date, 1998 data[1]

in New Zealand after 1994 is consistent with predictions, given its requirement that new drugs accept reference pricing and give a price cut relative to the prevailing RP, which was already the lowest price of established products in the class.

As an additional measure of availability of new molecules, table 1.2 lists the availability and mean launch lag of the forty-three new medical entities (NMEs) launched in the United States between 1991 and 1998, where launch lag is measured relative to a compound's first launch in any of these three countries or the United States.[19] Because Germany exempted new patented products from RP after 1996, we divide the sample into molecules launched before and after that date. For all three countries, the availability of these NMEs is less for NMEs launched post-1996 compared to the 1991–1995 period, which may partly reflect lags in diffusion combined with right-censored data. For New Zealand, however, there is a dramatic drop, from 50 percent of the pre-1996 molecules to 13 percent of the post-1996 molecules launched. The declines are less dramatic in Germany (from 93 percent to 73 percent) and the Netherlands (from 82 percent to 62 percent). The mean and median launch lags for introduction of these NMEs are lowest for Germany and highest for New Zealand. Thus, even for the limited subset of molecules that are introduced, launch lags are longer in the Netherlands and longest in New Zealand compared to Germany.

To test whether this reduced availability of drugs in New Zealand and, to a lesser extent, the Netherlands might be related to low RPs in these countries, figure 1.1 shows the median ratios of RPs and prices in the Netherlands and New Zealand, respectively, relative to Germany.

Table 1.2
Availability and launch lag (months) of new medical entities (NME) launched in the United States 1991–1998, as of 1998

		Total	Germany	The Netherlands	New Zealand
Availability					
NME 1991–1995		28	26	23	14
			93%	82%	50%
NME 1996–1998		15	11	10	2
			73%	67%	13%
Lag of available	Mean		5.8	6.8	19
molecules[a]	Median		0	1	12
	n		37	33	16

[a]Lag defined as the number of months after earliest of FDA date, launch in Germany, NL, or NZ.

Molecules are categorized by Country-specific launch date rather than Global launch date to reflect country-specific regulatory regimes. The sample of molecules is restricted to those available in both Germany and the comparison country.[20] Median rather than mean values are reported because means are very sensitive to outlier values. For the Netherlands relative to Germany, the median RP ratio increases from .75 for compounds launched before 1987 to 1.12 for compounds launched after 1994; the Netherlands/Germany price ratios follow a similar upward trend. Thus, for compounds launched under reference pricing, Dutch RPs and manufacturer prices are typically 7 to 12 percent higher than German prices as of 1998. For the post-1994 molecule cohort, the Dutch price ratios are lower than the RP ratios, which may reflect the constraints imposed by the Dutch Maximum Price Law, which capped prices for most molecules below their respective RPs and hence made the RPs nonbinding. In general, the finding of lower prices and RPs in Germany than the Netherlands for molecules launched after 1990 may reflect the stronger incentives for dynamic price competition in Germany due to the physician drug budgets. By increasing physicians' price sensitivity, these budgets created incentives for manufacturers to price below the initial RP levels, which permitted consequent downward revisions of RPs in Germany.

For New Zealand, by contrast, median RP ratios are over 40 percent lower than those in Germany, for three of the four time periods, whereas median prices range from 53 percent lower to 3 percent higher than those in Germany, with the lowest prices and RPs for the oldest cohort. Thus, in general, RPs and manufacturer prices are much lower in New Zealand than in Germany or the Netherlands, as expected given Pharmac's use of bargaining to negotiate cuts in prices and RPs as a condition for the entry of new products. The surprising exception is that post-1994 molecules are priced 3 percent higher on average in New Zealand than in Germany, although RPs are 35 percent lower. A plausible explanation is biased selection; that is, these newest molecules were launched in New Zealand only if they could charge a price comparable to European levels. This interpretation is consistent with the small number of post-1994 molecules launched in New Zealand compared to earlier cohorts, as shown in table 1.2.[21]

To test whether aggressive RP systems are biased disproportionately against relatively expensive drugs, figure 1.2 reports price and RP ratios for the Netherlands and New Zealand relative to Germany, with the sample of molecules divided based on the price distribution in

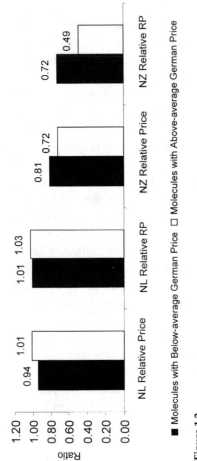

Figure 1.2
NL and NZ molecule prices and RPs relative to Germany, by German price, 1998.

Germany. We use Germany as the benchmark because it has the most molecules and because its price distribution is expected to reflect potential free market prices more closely. For the Netherlands, the median RPs are 1 to 3 percent higher than the German RPs for products in the lower and upper halves of the price distribution. For prices, the Netherlands' median price relatives are lower for molecules that are low-priced in Germany than for higher-priced molecules (0.94 versus 1.01). This finding suggests that the Dutch Maximum Price regulations were more binding for lower-priced molecules, possibly because generics are included in calculating the price ceiling. The Netherlands also has a higher percentage of the higher-price molecules: 71 percent of the high-price molecules compared to 57 percent of less-expensive molecules. This situation may reflect the greater incentives to launch higher-priced products due to relatively high reimbursement and/or early withdrawal of products with relatively low reimbursement.

In New Zealand, by contrast, RP levels are disproportionately lower for more expensive drugs than they are for less expensive drugs, and with greater compression of RPs for high-price rather than low-price drugs (0.49 versus 0.72) than for prices (0.72 versus 0.81). This suggests that manufacturers charge higher surcharges on more expensive products to partly make up for lower RPs. However, the bias against expensive products is also reflected in availability, with only 44 percent of the more expensive drugs available in New Zealand compared to 51 percent of the less expensive drugs.

In summary, Dutch RPs and prices were typically at or above German price and RP levels (except for the oldest cohort, which has prices and RPs below those in Germany). The smaller differential for prices reflects the Netherlands' regulated price ceilings based on foreign referencing that imposed stricter controls than did the ineffectual RP system (until the RPs were cut in 1999). Thus, the Dutch RP system failed to reduce manufacturer prices until additional, externally regulated controls were added in 1996. The relatively low price levels in Germany, together with other evidence of dynamic downward revisions of prices and RPs in Germany over time, were largely due to the global drug budget that placed physicians at risk for overruns, whereas the RP system created no incentives for manufacturers to set prices below the initial RP levels.

In New Zealand, Pharmac's requirement that new products offer a price below the prevailing RP as a condition of admission to reimbursement, thereby reducing the RP for existing products, succeeded in reducing RP levels to 51 percent of German levels for drugs launched from 1991 to 1994. It appears to be less effective for the post-1994 cohort of new drugs, but this may reflect selection bias: only 13 percent of the post-1996 cohort of new drugs was launched in New Zealand during our observation period, and presumably those that were launched did so because they were able to obtain a relatively high price. Moreover, in New Zealand relative prices are always higher than the relative RPs compared to Germany, and these differentials are greater for expensive products. Overall, these results confirm that New Zealand's RP system has set relatively low reimbursement levels, particularly for the newest drugs and the most expensive drugs. Many of these drugs are simply not available in New Zealand and for those that are available, patients on average face out-of-pocket surcharges.

Compression of Reimbursement Within Drug Classes
An important issue in defining RP systems is the degree of consensus about the substitutability of different drugs. A finding of consistency across countries in classification and relative RP levels for different drugs suggests broad clinical agreement about the relative merits of different molecules, even though the formal criteria differ across countries and absolute RP levels may differ. On the other hand, if the classification systems and relative RPs differ significantly across countries, this suggests either significant clinical disagreement in defining clusters or that budgetary concerns in practice override clinical judgment. Given the broader criteria for defining classes in New Zealand, we predict greater compression of RPs across drugs within a therapeutic category in New Zealand.

Although our data do not permit us to compare classification systems, we can compare the compression of reimbursement across molecules within each broad therapeutic category. The compression of RPs provides a bottom-line measure of the effect of the classification structure because a separate subgroup for improved products in a therapeutic category is relevant only to the extent that the RP for this subgroup differs from the RP for inferior products. Table 1.3 reports several measures of the compression of RPs across molecules within each therapeutic category (the sample is restricted to molecules that are available in all three countries).

The results are generally consistent with expectations. In most country-class cells, there is a considerable range in RPs. New Zealand has the lowest median and maximum RPs for eight of the nine therapeutic

Table 1.3
Measures of reimbursement dispersion within ATC2s based on molecule average, 1998 data[a]

ATC2	N	Mini-mum	Median	Maxi-mum	Max/min	Max − min	(Max − min)/median	Standard deviation
Germany								
A2	22	0.04	0.21	1.62	39.66	1.58	7.61	0.45
A10	13	0.03	0.10	0.56	16.56	0.53	5.42	0.14
C1	5	0.07	0.23	0.70	9.63	0.63	2.79	0.24
C3	26	0.04	0.12	0.61	16.83	0.58	4.79	0.12
C7	21	0.07	0.26	0.52	7.39	0.45	1.75	0.14
C8	14	0.11	0.33	0.73	6.49	0.61	1.88	0.18
C9	17	0.20	0.36	0.76	3.75	0.55	1.56	0.16
C10	20	0.07	0.39	0.89	12.76	0.82	2.09	0.23
N6	34	0.04	0.28	1.37	32.64	1.32	4.70	0.40
Median:		0.07	0.26	0.73	12.76	0.61	2.79	0.18
The Netherlands								
A2	14	0.07	0.70	1.72	24.92	1.65	2.34	0.56
A10	7	0.05	0.11	0.48	9.97	0.43	3.78	0.15
C1	3	0.07	0.09	0.32	4.73	0.25	2.93	0.14
C3	11	0.06	0.09	0.21	3.73	0.15	1.65	0.06
C7	17	0.07	0.22	0.59	8.53	0.52	2.39	0.13
C8	12	0.14	0.39	0.98	6.82	0.83	2.12	0.24
C9	14	0.24	0.55	0.88	3.72	0.64	1.17	0.18
C10	11	0.05	0.44	1.34	28.00	1.29	2.92	0.43
N6	22	0.04	0.21	1.32	35.53	1.28	6.08	0.43
Median:		0.07	0.22	0.88	8.53	0.64	2.39	0.18
New Zealand								
A2	13	0.00	0.16	0.83	547.60	0.82	5.01	0.27
A10	5	0.04	0.08	0.09	2.32	0.05	0.64	0.02
C1	3	0.02	0.03	0.14	6.69	0.12	4.18	0.07
C3	10	0.01	0.03	0.12	12.28	0.11	3.43	0.04
C7	12	0.01	0.05	0.28	26.52	0.27	5.56	0.09
C8	7	0.18	0.36	0.71	3.87	0.53	1.48	0.19
C9	9	0.10	0.17	0.71	7.17	0.61	3.63	0.19
C10	11	0.00	0.31	0.93	9306.17	0.93	3.04	0.27
N6	20	0.03	0.19	1.04	34.12	1.01	5.24	0.29
Median:		0.02	0.16	0.71	12.28	0.53	3.63	0.19

[a]Sample restricted to molecules with data available in all three countries.
Note: Shading indicates the lowest value for each cell across the three countries.

categories, and the lowest range and standard deviation for seven and six categories, respectively. The normalized range, defined as (maximum − minimum)/median, is lowest in New Zealand for only two of the nine categories, presumably because the low median offsets the high range. This is additional evidence that New Zealand's approach (using broad criteria for defining clusters and setting the RP at the lowest price in each class) has resulted in greater compression of RPs across molecules in a therapeutic category than has the less restrictive criteria used in the Netherlands and Germany. We estimated similar distributions using the product and the pack as the unit of analysis. Results were very similar to the molecule-level distributions reported in table 1.3.[22]

RPs, Prices, and Generic Competition
RP is often rationalized as a mechanism to stimulate competition (see, for example, Kletchko, Moore, and Jones 1995) because the payer pays the same price for all products in a cluster. The monopolistic competition model implies that firms that previously priced above the RP would likely reduce their prices to the RP, while firms that previously priced below the RP may increase their prices, leading to a convergence of prices on the RP. Dynamic downward pressure on prices is not expected except where other programs create incentives or constraints for pricing below the RP, such as Germany's physician drug budgets or New Zealand's requirement for price cuts from new entrants. Thus, the prediction is that, under RP, prices would be inversely related to the number of competitors in Germany and New Zealand but not in the Netherlands unless this effect was "imported" from pre-RP prices (which were the basis of the initial RP levels) or from foreign prices through the maximum price ceilings. Because our database is a half-year cross-section of prices, we cannot measure price changes in response to RP. Nevertheless, these 1998 data do reflect several years of experience under RP for all three countries.

Our multivariate analysis estimates reduced-form, quasi-hedonic equations for RP, price, and surcharge per unit for all products in our sample in each country. Standard hedonic price equations estimate the relationship between prices and product characteristics or cost factors that influence demand or marginal cost. Our regressions are quasi-hedonic because the perfect competition assumption of standard hedonic theory does not apply to pharmaceutical markets, which are imperfectly competitive and subject to regulation. Our equations therefore include measures of competition and indicators of regulatory regime in addition to product characteristics.

The quasi-hedonic estimating equation for the price of product i in molecule j in therapeutic class k can be written as follows:

$$P_{ijk} = \alpha_0 + \alpha_1 Z_{jk} + \alpha_2 N^g_j + \alpha_3 N^t_k + \alpha_4 R_{ij} \tag{1.1}$$

where Z_{jk} is a vector of product quality dimensions and other characteristics that are expected to influence demand, α_2 reflects the effect of the number of generic competitors N^g_j in molecule j, and α_3 reflects the effect of the number of therapeutic substitutes (other compounds) in class k (N^t_k). We predict α_2, $\alpha_3 < 0$, and $|\alpha_2| > |\alpha_3|$ if generic competition exerts greater downward pressure on prices than does therapeutic competition. R_{ij} is a vector of indicators for regulatory regime.

Because RPs are based on lagged manufacturer supply prices, RPs are expected to reflect the same product and market characteristics that affect prices. Surcharges are defined as the difference between the price and the RP; hence, the surcharge equations test for significant differences in coefficients between the RP and price equations.[23] We use the same specification but estimate separate equations for each country. This approach permits all coefficients to vary across countries and facilitates comparison of coefficients across countries. One exception is that the Parallel Import indicator is omitted from the New Zealand equations because there are no parallel imports in New Zealand.

Product Characteristics. Pharmaceutical prices are expected to depend on the value of the product to consumers and the extent of competition. We include several measures of product efficacy. A quadratic in Global molecule age (log), defined as months from the molecule's first launch in any of our sample countries, is included as a general proxy for product efficacy. Newer compounds are expected to have higher prices, assuming that they are clinically superior on average to older molecules. A dummy variable controls for herbal products and molecules that were launched before 1950, for which the IMS age data are imprecise. Strength, defined as grams of active ingredient per unit, is included as a proxy for product potency. The coefficient is expected to be positive, assuming that a stronger dose of a given compound has greater expected efficacy. Indicator variables are included for Retard, Liquid, and Transdermal formulations; regular tablets and capsules is the omitted category. Retard forms are expected to have higher prices, assuming that delayed release forms offer greater convenience to patients. Pack size (units per pack) is expected to be negatively related to price if economies of scale in packaging are passed on to consumers.

An Originator product indicator is included to test for brand loyalty. The coefficient is expected to be positive in the price equation but not in the subsidy equation if brand loyalty persists among physicians and/or patients, but RP systems do not reflect these differences. An indicator variable is included for parallel imports (PIs); the coefficient is expected to be negative in the price and subsidy equations if the savings from PIs is captured by payers. Measurement of this effect may be confounded, however, by nonrandom entry of PIs, that is, if products that attract PIs are disproportionately high-priced products. For example, omeprazole (Prilosec), which is priced well above average in Germany, has nine parallel import products, whereas most compounds have none; in the Netherlands, omeprazole has five parallel imports.

Indicator variables for three-digit Anatomical therapeutic classes (ATCs) are included to control for unmeasured differences in average product value by therapeutic category. The ACE inhibitors and angiotensin-II antagonists (C09) are omitted as the reference group.

Competition. We include three measures of competition: Generic Competitors measures the number of manufacturers in the molecule; Molecules in the three-digit ATC is a measure of therapeutic substitute compounds; and Products of other molecules in the four-digit ATC is a measure of the intensity of competition within the therapeutic substitute molecules. In Germany, RPs and prices are expected to be negatively related to the number of generic and therapeutic competitors because RP levels were initially set lower in classes with more competitors and because Germany's drug budgets made physicians price-sensitive, thus creating incentives for price competition that enabled subsequent downward revisions of RPs.

In the Netherlands, RPs are expected to be inversely related to the number of competitors only to the extent that the 1991 price structure on which they were based reflected competition. For prices, the Dutch RP system did not encourage competition in list prices; hence, prices are expected to be related to the number of competitors only to the extent that this was imported through the maximum price caps. In New Zealand, RPs are expected to be inversely related to the number of generic and therapeutic competitors because of Pharmac's requirement that new entrants to a class give a price cut relative to the existing

RP. The estimated relationship may be biased by reverse causation, however, if manufacturers were more likely to introduce products to classes with higher RPs. In all three countries, the kinked demand model predicts greater price competition at prices above the RP than below the RP. Because we lack the data to identify these ranges separately, the estimates in table 1.4 reflect the average effects over the full range of prices.

Regulatory variables.   Our tests for differential regulatory effects focus on the year of launch of the molecule in each country because launch prices establish the base from which prices adjust over time, with price increases rarely permitted in regulated markets. We use molecule rather than product launch date because generic and other later entrants in an established molecule are constrained by the price and reimbursement of the originator product in the molecule under both RP and competitive regimes. We include variables indicating molecules launched in the country from 1987 to 1990, from 1991 to 1994, and after 1994. The last two categories roughly identify compounds launched under RP; their coefficients are expected to be negative if RP systems are biased against new products. The omitted category is products launched before 1987 and hence before RP. These older compounds are likely to be off-patent by 1998, but the effect of generic entry should be captured by our measure of generic competitors.[24]

In all regressions we include an indicator for products that are not reference-priced (Not-RP). Because these products are not randomly chosen but are mostly new products or products that could not be clustered, this variable does not identify the effects of reference pricing. For Germany, where products outside the RP system were usually fully reimbursed, the coefficient of the Not-RP indicator is expected to be positive in the subsidy equation if RP lowers reimbursement levels on average. The surcharge for these observations is zero by definition. For New Zealand, non-RP molecules typically are not reimbursed, so the coefficient of the Not-RP indicator is expected to be negative in the subsidy equation, positive in the surcharge equation. For the Netherlands, some non-RP products are reimbursed; others are not.[25]

Empirical Results.   Table 1.4 reports estimates of the price, subsidy, and surcharge regressions, with the pack as the unit of observation. Estimates using the product as the unit of analysis are very similar

Table 1.4
Effects of regulation and competition on price, reimbursement (RP), and surcharge per standard unit, pack level[a]

	Germany			The Netherlands			New Zealand		
	Reimbursement	Price	Surcharge	Reimbursement	Price	Surcharge	Reimbursement	Price	Surcharge
Molecule age (ln)	1.962	1.099	-0.191	1.526	1.430	-0.088	1.061	1.581	0.097
	(5.44)***	(3.21)***	(2.71)***	(3.74)***	(3.79)***	(2.05)**	(1.05)	(1.92)*	(1.04)
Molecule age (ln) squared	-0.301	-0.170	0.031	-0.271	-0.258	0.010	-0.171	-0.223	-0.010
	(8.73)***	(5.24)***	(3.79)***	(7.09)***	(7.29)***	(2.63)***	(1.74)*	(2.80)***	(1.08)
Molecule herbal or introduced before 1950	0.448	-0.033	-0.205	0.852	0.817	-0.011	1.350	1.012	0.090
	(2.26)**	(0.20)	(3.20)***	(2.42)**	(2.53)**	(0.36)	(2.08)**	(2.69)***	(1.47)
Molecule introduced 1987–1990	0.287	0.764	0.075	0.133	0.178	-0.015	0.227	0.238	0.035
	(2.47)**	(7.38)***	(3.22)***	(1.42)	(2.03)**	(1.27)	(1.81)*	(2.08)**	(1.71)*
Molecule introduced 1991–1994	-0.027	0.580	0.007	-0.451	-0.377	0.002	-0.120	-0.216	-0.022
	(0.21)	(5.01)***	(0.10)	(3.24)***	(2.92)***	(0.13)	(0.51)	(0.89)	(0.38)
Molecule introduced after 1994	-0.510	0.380	0.153	-0.952	-0.866	-0.030	0.062	0.012	-0.008
	(1.57)	(1.30)	(3.17)***	(3.93)***	(3.76)***	(0.92)	(0.17)	(0.04)	(0.13)
Originator product (dv)	-0.055	0.307	0.097	0.208	0.191	0.001	-0.164	-0.003	0.017
	(0.92)	(5.30)***	(5.03)***	(1.82)*	(2.07)**	(0.10)	(1.78)*	(0.04)	(1.75)*
Parallel import	0.044	0.285	0.055	0.210	0.095	-0.040	0.000	0.000	0.000
	(1.11)	(8.27)***	(4.88)***	(1.94)*	(1.10)	(4.33)***	(.)	(.)	(.)
Genetic competitors	-0.010	-0.010	-0.001	-0.016	-0.007	0.000	-0.273	-0.149	0.006
	(3.61)***	(4.16)***	(1.21)	(1.99)**	(0.99)	(0.11)	(6.35)***	(3.85)***	(0.72)

Table 1.4
(continued)

	Germany			The Netherlands			New Zealand		
	Reim-bursement	Price	Sur-charge	Reim-bursement	Price	Sur-change	Reim-bursement	Price	Sur-change
Molecules in atc3	0.005	-0.002	0.000	-0.005	0.001	0.004	0.188	0.007	-0.008
	(0.26)	(0.14)	(0.10)	(0.09)	(0.02)	(2.29)**	(2.82)***	(0.16)	(0.79)
Products of other molecules in atc4	-0.003	-0.003	-0.001	0.007	0.005	-0.001	-0.145	-0.045	0.006
	(1.26)	(1.92)*	(1.40)	(1.99)**	(1.50)	(3.26)***	(4.84)***	(1.96)*	(1.13)
Constant	-3.732	-2.999	0.202	-1.960	-1.807	0.190	-1.311	-1.341	0.005
	(3.91)***	(3.30)***	(1.13)	(1.78)*	(1.79)*	(1.59)	(0.48)	(0.59)	(0.02)
Observations	7174	7174	7174	1688	1688	1688	387	387	387
R-squared	0.53	0.51	0.45	0.75	0.79	0.16	0.93	0.72	0.58

[a]t-statistics with robust standard errors clustered by product. Regressions also include variables for form, strength, and pack size, and indicator variables for not reference priced, therapeutic class, and imputed RPs.
*p <.10 **p <.05 ***p <.01

and are not reported here. Table 1.4 reports *t* statistics based on robust standard errors and adjusted for clustering across packs within a product.

The quadratic in Global Molecule Age (a proxy for product efficacy) implies that price and subsidy initially increase and then decrease with molecule age. These effects are significant for price, subsidy, and surcharge in Germany and the Netherlands, but only for price in New Zealand. The estimates imply that price and subsidy are highest for molecules launched within the most recent two years and then decline for older molecules, as expected under the hypothesis that older products are generally perceived to be less effective and thus are sold at lower prices and receive lower subsidies. (Note that these estimates control for the number of competitors, which increases with molecule age and is a control for patent status.) In Germany and the Netherlands, surcharges are also significantly higher for newer products, reaching a maximum for two-year-old products in Germany and seven-year-old products in the Netherlands. This implies that RP offers lower subsidy differentials for new products than the price differentials that are supported by the market.

The regulatory variables imply that, after controlling for Global Molecule Age and Number of Competitors, in all three countries RP subsidies for new compounds were similar to the subsidies for compounds launched prior to 1987 (which were presumably mostly off-patent by 1998). By contrast, subsidies for compounds launched from 1987 to 1990, that is, compounds that were probably still on-patent in 1998 but launched prior to RP, received higher subsidies. In the Netherlands, molecules launched after 1991, i.e., under the RP system, received lower subsidies than did molecules launched before 1987, with most negative effects for the most recent, post-1994 compounds. The pattern is similar in Germany, although significance levels are lower. Specifically, in Germany, the post-1991 compounds have subsidies comparable to pre-1987 compounds, whereas the compounds launched from 1987 to 1990, which would primarily be compounds that were launched before the RP system but that are still on-patent in 1998, receive the highest subsidies. Similarly, in New Zealand, the more recent compounds launched under RP have subsidies similar to the pre-1987 compounds, whereas compounds that were launched from 1987 to 1990, before the adoption of reference pricing, have higher subsidies, prices, and surcharges.

In Germany the newest, post-1994 molecules have the highest surcharges, whereas surcharges are not related to regulatory regime in the

Netherlands, presumably because of the price controls. In New Zealand, prices, surcharges, and subsidies are highest for compounds launched prior to RP.

Originator products do not receive higher subsidies than do generics in Germany, consistent with the intent of generic referencing, and in New Zealand originator products receive 16 percent lower subsidies. In the Netherlands, originators receive roughly 21 percent higher subsidies than generics. Because these coefficient estimates reflect both between-molecule and within-molecule differences, even the Netherlands' estimate of a small positive differential is not necessarily inconsistent with the expectation that RP eliminates subsidy differentials for originator versions of a given pack, compared to generic versions of that same pack, as predicted under generic referencing. By contrast, originator price differentials over generics are significant in Germany (31 percent originator price differential) and the Netherlands (19 percent originator differential). Out-of-pocket surcharges are significantly higher on originator products in Germany and also New Zealand, where they are small in magnitude on average. In the Netherlands, the originator surcharge differential is insignificant, possibly because of the maximum price constraints.

In Germany, parallel imports do not receive significantly different subsidies but they do charge higher prices and have positive surcharges. In fact, the similarity between the PI coefficient (.285) and the originator coefficient (.307) suggests that, in Germany, PIs simply shadow-price the originator products, yielding little savings to payers or patients, which is additional evidence of weak incentives for price competition under Germany's RP system. Not surprisingly, the PI market share was small in Germany. In the Netherlands, the PI coefficient is similar to the originator coefficient for subsidies but smaller for price; thus, the PI surcharge is negative but small in magnitude. Taken at face value, these results indicate little savings to payers from PIs. These conclusions are tentative because the PI coefficients may be upward biased if PIs are more likely to enter for high-priced products.

The evidence on competition is generally consistent with the kinked demand model, as adapted to fit each country's RP system. The number of Generic Competitors is negatively related to both subsidies and prices in both Germany and New Zealand. In Germany, the estimates imply that each additional competitor leads to only a 1 percent reduction in subsidy or price. This small marginal effect of additional generics is consistent with weak incentives for generic competition under RP in Germany. It is also not surprising because most generics in Germany are branded; hence, they compete on brand image and reputation, which contrasts with unbranded generics that predominate in the United States and compete predominantly on price. In New Zealand, the marginal effect of an additional generic competitor is 27 percent for subsidy and 15 percent for price. These effects presumably reflect the requirement that new generic entrants offer a reduction in price and RP as a condition of reimbursement. In the Netherlands, the number of generic competitors has a significant but small (1.6 percent) effect on subsidy but no significant effect on price, which is expected given the lack of incentives to compete on list price. The number of products in substitute molecules has an economically small negative effect on subsidies in Germany and on surcharges in the Netherlands, but a larger and more significant negative effect in New Zealand, with a more negative effect for subsidy than for price, again possibly because of the regulatory requirement that new entrants accept lower prices and hence reduce the RPs for the entire class. Thus, the evidence on the effects of generic competition under RP is consistent for intramolecular and closely related generic competitors: by itself, RP does not encourage generic competitors to compete on price. Downward price pressure occurs only when this is enforced through regulation, as in New Zealand, or where other institutional factors outside the RP system create incentives for price competition, such as drug budgets in Germany or off-list discounting to pharmacists in the Netherlands.

Similarly, there is no evidence of price competition from therapeutic substitutes in any of the three countries. On the contrary, in New Zealand subsidy levels are significantly positively related to the number of molecules in the ATC3. These estimates may reflect endogeneity bias if new compounds enter the New Zealand market only if they can obtain a relatively high subsidy level, as shown in table 1.3.

Other product characteristics included in the estimating equations but not reported here generally have the expected signs. Subsidy and price are generally positively related to strength (grams of active ingredient) per dose and negatively related to pack size. Retard forms have significantly higher subsidies and prices than regular tablets (the omitted category), with similar magnitudes in all three countries. This finding suggests that manufacturers apply standard markups for these more costly forms. For transdermal forms, Germany has significantly higher subsidies, whereas New Zealand's subsidies do not differentiate between transdermal and standard oral forms. Products that are not reference-priced are generally not reimbursed in New Zealand, which is reflected in a large negative coefficient on the Not-RP indicator in the subsidy equation. By contrast, in the price equation, the Not-RP indicator is positive, indicating that these are relatively high-priced products.

The subsidy coefficients for several of the therapeutic category indicators are statistically significant, relative to the omitted category (ACE inhibitors), but coefficient magnitudes and even signs differ across countries. This tends to confirm the earlier evidence of a lack of consistent evaluation across countries of the relative merits of different products and/or that budget imperatives override clinical judgments.

VI. Conclusions on Effects of RP on Availability, Subsidies, and Prices

This evidence on the impact of reference pricing is broadly consistent with predictions given the differences in system design across our three countries. We find that New Zealand's RP system (which is most comprehensive, has the broadest classes, and uses monopsony power to obtain price reductions) is associated with significantly reduced availability of new products, particularly for more expensive compounds. Availability is also somewhat reduced in the Netherlands.

In all three countries, subsidies for molecules launched in the post-RP period are comparable to subsidies for (mostly off-patent) compounds launched before 1987 and are lower than subsidies for (mostly on-patent) compounds launched in the 1987–1990 period immediately prior to RP. These estimates control for cohort therapeutic effects and the number of competitors. Compared to older compounds, surcharges for the more recent drugs are positive in Germany, implying some willingness of consumers to pay more for newer products than was reflected in subsidy levels. Surcharges are negative in the Netherlands, but because both prices and RPs were set by regulation, this provides no evidence of market willingness to pay. In New Zealand, surcharges do not appear to be differentially higher on new products, but these conclusions are tentative because of small numbers.

Although a major objective of RP systems is to stimulate competition, there is no evidence of competition among therapeutic substitutes in any of the three countries. Although both subsidies and prices are inversely related to the number of generic competitors, magnitudes are small in both the Netherlands and Germany and may reflect other factors: physician drug budgets in Germany and, in the Netherlands, influences imported from the pre-RP era or from other countries through external referencing. In New Zealand, subsidies and, to a lesser extent, price are significantly negatively related to the number of generic competitors, but this finding reflects the regulatory requirement of price cuts from new entrants. This failure of generic referencing to stimulate competition in these three countries reflects the details of their system design: in particular, the regulation of pharmacy margins and weak incentives for pharmacists to substitute cheaper products. The exception is the Netherlands, where competition did occur but is not observable in these data on list prices because it took the form of discounts off list price, which yielded savings to pharmacies, not to payers, until the discounts were clawed back. An important conclusion is that the effects of RP in any country will depend critically on the structure of pharmacy incentives to substitute cheaper products. We discuss this further below when we consider the effects of adopting RP in the United States.

The evidence from regression analysis, that therapeutic referencing has not stimulated dynamic competition, is consistent with the kinked demand model of manufacturer response to RP. This conclusion is also supported by other circumstantial evidence, that all three countries found it necessary to adopt additional measures to control prices. In particular, the Netherlands adopted maximum prices based on foreign prices because their internal RP system had not stimulated dynamic competition as intended, and the resulting regulated prices made the RPs irrelevant for many products. In 2001, Germany mandated that pharmacies increase substitution of PIs and cheaper generics where available. Thus, Germany's RP system alone did not stimulate significant generic competition, which is not surprising because it gave no incentive to pharmacists to substitute cheaper products. New Zealand has used additional measures—requiring a price cut from new entrants and tendering—to enforce dynamic price competition. This has achieved lower prices, particularly on relatively expensive new compounds, but at the cost of reduced availability of these new compounds. In conclusion, both theory and empirical evidence support the conclusion that reference pricing, as structured in these three countries, did not deliver its main intended benefit of stimulating competition between substitute products except when it was implemented with aggressive monopsony power, as in New Zealand.

VII.   Reference Pricing as Efficient Insurance Benefit Design

Standard models of optimal insurance coverage focus on the trade-off between risk spreading and cost control in the context of moral hazard; medical services are usually implicitly assumed to be competitively supplied at prices equal to marginal cost. While the risk-spreading versus cost-control trade-off is also relevant to pharmaceutical benefit design, the optimal insurance structure for drugs must also consider the effects of reimbursement on drug prices and hence on manufacturers' incentives for innovation and provider/patient incentives for substitution between products. A formal model of optimal drug coverage is beyond the scope of this paper. In this section, we draw on existing models to suggest conclusions about the efficiency and equity of RP compared to alternatives such as a proportional co-insurance rate or a formulary with tiered copayments.

Standard models of optimal insurance conclude that, in an ideal world where the insurer has perfect information about the patient's condition and the appropriate treatment, the insurance payment would be an indemnity payment equal to the cost of treatment, and moral hazard would not exist. More realistically, when the insurer cannot observe the patient's condition and therefore treatment is determined by the physician/patient team subject to moral hazard, optimal insurance coverage (assuming reliance on demand management) involves a trade-off between risk spreading and lower premium payments (Pauly 1968, Zeckhauser 1970, Ma and Riordan 2002). Specifically, the optimal patient cost share for different conditions is greater, when the demand for treatment is more price elastic (Ma and Riordan 2002).

Applying this result to the RP context of patient heterogeneity in their response to different drugs, the optimal patient copayment schedule is likely to require some cost sharing between the patient and the insurer for the incremental cost of more expensive drugs, with the patient paying a larger share of the incremental cost as demand becomes more price elastic. RP pays an indemnity equal to the cheapest drug in a class, with 100 percent patient cost sharing for the incremental cost of more expensive drugs. Generic referencing is consistent with optimal insurance coverage for generically equivalent compounds because these products are required by regulation to be bioequivalent. Thus, differential patient response is generally not an issue. For therapeutic substitutes that differ in their effects for different patients, however, RP is unlikely to provide the optimal trade-off between risk spreading and cost control for patients who do not respond to the cheaper drug. RP is likely to be inferior to a co-insurance rate, which would provide some risk protection for the incremental cost of more expensive drugs for these patients. RP is also likely to be inferior to a tiered formulary, which would typically include several drugs on the preferred tier, even if they are priced differently, if patients are heterogeneous in their response to the different compounds in a class.

Similarly, from the perspective of equity, if patients differ in their response to drugs due to genetics, comorbidities, or other factors, and if the objective is to use public funds to ensure that everyone has a uniform basic level of care, then equity requires higher subsidies to higher-priced drugs if these are needed by some patients to achieve the target care level. If all drugs in a class are reimbursed at the price of the cheapest or most widely tolerated drug in the class, patients with comorbidities and those taking several other drugs—who may also be the sickest patients—may be most likely to face surcharges to obtain a drug that they can tolerate. By analogy, defined contribution insurance plans would pay risk-adjusted subsidies to sicker patients to enable them to buy the same basic care that healthy patients can buy with lower subsidies. By fully subsidizing only the cheapest product in a class, RP systems fail to risk-adjust the subsidy rate and thus do not enable patients for whom the cheapest drug is ineffective to achieve the same outcomes as other patients for whom the cheapest drug *is* effective.

Optimal insurance coverage for drugs should also take into account the effects of the subsidy structure on prices to suppliers and hence on incentives for innovation. Assume that the term and structure of patents are optimally set and that the price differential between on-patent and generic drugs is optimal before insurance. If insurance with therapeutic RP is introduced with a classification system that ignores patents, it effectively gives a full subsidy to generics but a zero subsidy to the patent-induced price differentials of on-patent drugs. This raises the relative out-of-pocket price of on-patent drugs faced by patients. This may lead manufacturers of on-patent drugs to reduce their prices if demand is highly elastic above the RP. But in any case, revenues of on-patent products will decline relative to revenues for generics, and incentives for innovation are reduced, particularly for drugs that offer improved treatments within existing categories, which are most likely to be subject to RP. By contrast, insurance with a fixed co-insurance rate or a tiered formulary would imply some insurance coverage of the on-patent price differential.

In practice, the optimal insurance share of the price differential between on-patent drugs and old generics depends on the incremental value of the innovation and on whether the patent structure is in fact optimal. Whether current patent protection is excessive, suboptimal, or just right cannot be determined a priori. But if the current rate of innovation is considered about right, then therapeutic RP, which reduces effective patent life for all but the first entrant in a new class, would reduce incentives for R&D to develop improved therapies within existing classes and result in suboptimal innovation compared to the status quo mix of proportional co-insurance and tiered copayment structures.[26] This conclusion still holds if both the generic and the on-patent drug are subject to a fixed copayment. This interaction between insurance coverage and incentives for innovation is another reason why the defined contribution approach to subsidizing insurance breaks down when applied to drugs. Insurance plans do not incur large fixed costs of R&D and rarely generate patentable innovations. Thus, patents are not relevant to the design of optimal subsidies for insurance coverage. By contrast, given the large fixed costs of R&D (both absolutely and as a percentage of total costs) and the importance of patents for innovator drugs, the optimal subsidy structure for pharmaceuticals cannot ignore the effects on incentives for innovation.

If RPs have a significant influence over manufacturer prices, as the theory and evidence above suggest, then RPs can influence price signals and hence efficiency of resource use. In particular, because the RP for different products is not necessarily differentiated based on their relative effectiveness, RP can distort prescribing choices. Appropriate incentives for resource use and for innovation require that compounds that are less effective or that require a longer course of treatment to achieve a given outcome should be reimbursed less per daily dose than more effective drugs or drugs that require fewer days or doses to achieve the same outcome. In practice, cost-effectiveness criteria are not used rigorously to set RPs. Typically, the RP applies to the daily dose of each drug in a class, regardless of differences in effects or required duration of treatment. By contrast, both a proportional co-insurance and a tiered copayment structure can easily tailor differences in reimbursement to reflect differences in efficacy. For example, a higher-priced but more effective drug could be on the preferred tier of a PBM formulary and receive a higher reimbursement than a cheaper but less cost-effective, inferior drug. We don't suggest that PBMs consider only cost-effectiveness and not budget costs in designing their formularies. The point is simply that the tiered formulary structure can easily reimburse different drugs in proportion to their differing effectiveness, and this sends appropriate signals for prescribing choices and for R&D. By contrast, RP systems tend to set equal reimbursement rates per daily dose for different drugs, regardless of differences in efficacy, which sends distorted signals for prescribing and for R&D.

VIII.   Implications for the United States

Reference pricing has been proposed for a Medicare drug benefit in the United States under the assumption that this benefit would be delivered by a single monopoly PBM in each geographic area (Huskamp et al. 2000, and more generally, Kanavos and Reinhardt 2003). If RP is simply an option that can be used by competing PBMs, then the use of monopsony power would be more limited and competitive forces would contrain its use to classes where drugs are highly interchangeable for most people. In fact, the limited evidence from private-sector PBM experience with RP suggests that the classes for which there was sufficient clinical consensus to adopt RP accounted for only roughly 30 percent of total ingredient cost. Despite a roughly 25 percent shifting from nonpreferred to preferred agents, estimated savings to the plan were only 1 percent of total drug spending (Sanders 2001).

RP would potentially play a larger role if PBMs are constrained from using tiered or otherwise restrictive formularies, which is likely if each area is served by only one PBM to avoid problems of risk selection. Huskamp et al. (2000) propose that PBMs periodically compete for the franchise in a particular area, but the successful bidder in each area would serve the entire area. In that case, seniors would have no choice of PBM, so the single monopoly PBM would probably be required to offer all drugs on an open formulary with a standard co-insurance or copayment rate, rather than on a tiered formulary typically offered by PBMs in the private sector. Such restrictions would eliminate the ability of PBMs to negotiate discounts from manufacturers in return for preferred formulary status, which would deprive them of their major tool for controlling drug prices. As an alternative, Huskamp et al. (2000) propose reference pricing. RP could also result as the drug product analogy of an "any willing provider" requirement that has been proposed for the participation of pharmacies in a Medicare drug benefit.

Although none of these proposals provide a detailed outline of how RP might work for Medicare, to achieve significant savings, it would have to include on-patent products, presumably with off-patent products, and exclude only first-in-class new products, as in the Netherlands and New Zealand. It would also presumably be a single national system. What does experience from these countries and from the U.S. system of RP for off-patent medicines tell us about how such a system might work in practice?

First, it is critical to distinguish between drugs in classes with only on-patent originator drugs versus classes that include generic versions of off-patent drugs. Presumably most new classes would start off as on-patent-only but would become mixed (on- and off-patent drugs) over time. For the on-patent-only classes, if the RP is set at the lowest price in the class, other prices would likely drop to the RP, except that some surcharges might remain for clearly differentiated products. There would be little incentive for dynamic price competition below the initial RP, however, unless the government agent used its monopsony power to demand price cuts from new entrants, as in New Zealand.[27]

Competitive bidding would probably not be an effective strategy unless winning bidders get some preferential placement on the formulary, which is precluded by the assumption of an open, nontiered formulary. With an open, nontiered formulary, each firm has little incentive to bid a low price ex ante because this would just increase the probability that the RP is low without increasing that firm's expected market share (because other competitors could reduce the prices to the RP once it had been set). Thus, an open formulary requirement eliminates a payer's ability to negotiate discounts. One possible outcome is that the Medicare RP system might take competitive bids and, following the lead of many state Medicaid programs, adopt prior authorization requirements for drugs that do not match the lowest bid price. This is a restrictive formulary in all but name. If firms still failed to bid low under this approach, the Medicare RP system might simply require that all firms give a specified discount off their private-sector prices or face prior authorization requirements, which is the approach adopted by many state Medicaid programs. This approach would achieve lower prices but through the exercise of monopsony power, not through competitive forces operating under the RP system as envisaged by proponents of the RP approach. Thus, unless an RP system exploits its monopsony power, it would be less effective at achieving competitive controls on prices than would PBMs that use tiered formularies because the tiered formularies enable the PBM to negotiate competitive discounts in return for moderate increases in market share. This conclusion that RP without either monopsony power or some formulary restrictions would be ineffective at controlling prices of on-patent drugs is limited, however, to classes with on-patent products only.

For mixed classes that include both on-patent molecules and off-patent molecules with generic products, the effect of RP on prices of the on-patent products could be dramatic, assuming that pharmacy incentives remain the same as under current maximum allowable charge (MAC) programs. Here, the experience of other countries with RP systems is misleading because their structure has been far less successful at stimulating generic competition than has the U.S. approach to generic referencing. Three factors contribute to greater generic competition under U.S. MAC programs than under RP in the countries studied. First, the default rule in the United States is that pharmacists can substitute a generic for a brand unless the physician expressly writes "brand required." Second, U.S. pharmacists have incentives to substitute the cheapest generic available because they capture the difference between the MAC reimbursement and the drug acquisition cost, whereas pharmacists in countries with regulated margins typically earn less if they dispense a lower-priced product. U.S. pharmacists' ability to profit from dispensing cheaper generics makes their demand highly price-elastic, which in turn gives generic manufacturers an incentive to compete on price. Third, payers in the United States capture much of the savings from generic competition by periodically reducing the MAC based on audits of actual acquisition prices. Lowering the MAC triggers another round of generic price competition as generic manufacturers seek to increase their market share by offering larger margins in pharmacies. If a Medicare RP required that RPs be fixed for a year, as proposed by Huskamp et al. (2000), more of the savings from generic competition would accrue to pharmacists rather than to payers, as in the Netherlands, and generic prices and reimbursement might decline somewhat less rapidly over time than they do currently under the more flexible MAC systems used by competing PBMs.

Assuming that a Medicare RP system would be structured to mimic roughly U.S. MAC programs for generics, this could have a devastating effect on revenues for on-patent products in the same class. For example, if generic prices are on average, say, 20 percent of originator prices, then the reimbursement for on-patent products would fall by 80 percent once the first molecule in the class goes off-patent. If an on-patent drug in a mixed class maintained its price, patients would face an out-of-pocket cost equal to the brand–generic price differential, which would likely be significantly higher than surcharges faced by patients in other RP countries and significantly higher than the differential surcharge on nonpreferred drugs under tiered formularies.[28] Many patients would presumably ask their physicians to switch them to the off-patent generic; others might ask their physicians to seek a special exemption from the surcharge, which would entail administrative costs. If demand is sufficiently elastic, originator prices would drop to the RP. Because of either lower prices or volumes or both, on-patent originator products would experience significant loss of revenue and effective loss of patent protection once the first drug in a class went off-patent.

Thus if therapeutic RP were combined with the more competitive generic RP system in the U.S., the negative effect on revenues of on-patent drugs in mixed classes would likely be greater than in the Netherlands or New Zealand, where generic competition is weaker. Although in principle this effect of RP would apply only to the roughly 40 percent of sales accounted for by seniors, in practice private payers and Medicaid would likely demand similar prices to those obtained by Medicare. Thus, the reduction in revenues would likely apply to the entire U.S. market. Because the United States accounts for over 50 percent of global pharmaceutical revenues and a larger share of profits, the effect on incentives for R&D could thus be significant. This significant effect of RP in mixed classes does not depend on a Medicare RP system exploiting its monopsony power. It results solely from classifying on-patent drugs with off-patent drugs in the U.S. context, in which there is aggressive generic competition as a result of the incentive structure for pharmacists.

The effect of RP in the United States on the availability of new products will also be very different from other countries' experiences. Given the dominant U.S. share of the global market, it seems likely that manufacturers would rationally choose to launch new drugs because the foregone sales from not launching would be far higher than in a small market such as New Zealand. Thus, RP applied in the United States would probably not affect the availability of new drugs that are already far along in the development process (for which most fixed costs are already sunk). By contrast, the long-term effect of RP in the United

States on the number of new drugs developed would be far greater than in other countries. A significant reduction in expected revenues in the U.S. market would significantly reduce expected global revenues and hence reduce incentives for companies to develop new drugs. These effects might not be evident for at least 5 to 10 years, assuming that the main R&D cuts would occur for drugs still at the preclinical or phase 1 stage, (for which significant investments must still be made). The evidence from other countries cannot inform analysis of these effects given the much larger U.S. share of global sales. If a New Zealand–style approach to obtaining price cuts were applied to on-patent classes, in addition to classifying on-patent with off-patent products, the reduction in expected returns to R&D and hence in incentives for new R&D investment could be very large.

Appendix 1.1:   Internal Reference Pricing, External Referencing, Price Regulation, and Formularies

Internal Reference Pricing
Internal referencing pricing systems set a common reimbursement level for different products in a designated group, with the reference price usually based on some low price in the distribution of manufacturer prices for the group of drugs. Thus, internal reference pricing compares prices across different products within a given country; its goal is to encourage price competition among manufacturers, but prices are not regulated.

External Referencing
External referencing refers to systems that limit the price and reimbursement of a specific product in one country by referring to the price of that same product in another country. This approach limits the manufacturer's ability to price-discriminate across countries for a given product but does not directly seek to promote competition between products. External referencing is used in many countries, including Italy, Canada, Belgium, Spain, and the Netherlands the latter also uses internal referencing.[29]

Price Regulation
In pure price regulatory systems such as those in France or Italy, the maximum reimbursable price is also the maximum that the manufacturer can charge. This regulated price may be based on external referencing to

foreign prices for the same drug or prices of similar products on the market. Although this latter approach resembles internal RP superficially, it differs in several important respects. First, the new drug may receive a higher reimbursement price if it can show significant therapeutic advantage over existing products. Second, the cross-product comparisons usually apply only to setting the launch price of the new drug; post-launch prices are not systematically reviewed and revised when a new product enters the class. Third, in pure price regulatory schemes, the manufacturer is not permitted to charge more than the regulated price.

Formularies

Tiered formularies used by pharmacy benefit managers (PBMs) in the United States categorize compounds by therapeutic category. Within each therapeutic category, however, the reimbursement paid to manufacturers and the copayments charged to patients can differ based on cost effectiveness and other factors that the PBM uses to classify products as generics, preferred brands, and nonpreferred brands. Corresponding copayment rates are, say, $5 for a generic, $15 for a preferred brand, and $30 for a nonpreferred brand. Because PBMs can shift utilization toward preferred products, they can negotiate discounts from manufacturers in return for granting preferred status to their products. Thus, unlike RP, in a tiered formulary, different compounds within a therapeutic category are commonly reimbursed at different rates. For example, if drug A is more effective than drug B in the same class, drug A can be reimbursed at a higher price and still be on the preferred tier, provided that it is equally or more cost-effective than drug B at the higher price. The reimbursement for on-patent products in a class does not immediately fall to generic levels when the patent expires on one molecule in the class. If, say, compound B is off-patent and has generic competitors, the PBM may encourage generic substitution by paying only for the generic version of compound B or placing brand B in the nonpreferred tier with a much higher copayment. But brand A, which is still on-patent, may be on the preferred tier and receive a higher reimbursement than generic B if brand A offers some advantages over generic B. Patient copayment differentials are also more open-ended under RP than in the tiered copay model.

Notes

This study was supported by a grant from Wyeth. We would like to thank IMS Health for providing the data. The views expressed are those of the authors.

1. IMS Health (IMS) is a global market research company based in Plymouth Meeting, Pa.

2. For more detail on Germany, see Ulrich and Wille (1996); for the Netherlands, see Rigter (1994) and de Vos (1996); for New Zealand, see Kletchko, Moore, and Jones (1995) and Woodfield (2001); for analysis of reference pricing in general, see Lopez-Casasnovas and Puig-Junoy (2001), Jonsson (2001), and Danzon (2001).

3. In 1999, the pharmaceutical industry challenged the right of the BKK to set RP levels as a violation of German and European Union (EU) competition law. In 2001, the federal government assumed these functions.

4. Most generics in Germany are branded, and physicians frequently prescribe the specific brand of generic. By contrast, in the United States, generics are not branded; the pharmacist is authorized to substitute unless the physician requires the brand; and because U.S. pharmacists can profit from the margin between the reimbursement and the acquisition cost, pharmacists have strong financial incentives to substitute cheap generics, which in turn creates incentives for generic manufacturers to compete on price.

5. From 1989 to 1993, products under RP were exempt from the DM3 copayment that applied to non-RP drugs. In 1993, all drugs were subject to a DM3/5/7 copayment structure initially based on the price, later on the pack size.

6. An incentive for manufacturers to price below the RP could exist if physicians are imperfectly informed about the RP and therefore tend to choose the cheapest products to reduce the risk of a patient surcharge and, in Germany, to avoid the obligation to explain the need for a surcharged product.

7. The five criteria were (1) same mechanism of action; (2) used for the same indication, based on actual use, not the official product labeling; (3) similar route of administration (for example, parenteral forms are grouped separately from oral forms of the same compound); (4) intended for the same age group; and (5) no significant differences in clinical effects, desirable or undesirable, for *all* patients. This broadened the earlier definition, which permitted a separate class if the clinical differences affected only some patients.

8. To inform patients, some pharmacists reportedly simply post a notice advising that substitution will occur unless the patient requests otherwise.

9. The average is an (unweighted) average price per day at the ex-wholesaler level, using the package size with the lowest unit cost in each country, including all originator and generic products (excluding parallel imports).

10. A full analysis of the effects of RP on manufacturers would include the probability that a compound is launched; the probability that a product is reference-priced and the determination of RP level; the manufacturer's price response and patient surcharge, conditional on RP; unit sales volume and market shares; and dynamic evolution of RPs, prices, and quantities over time.

11. Parallel trade refers to arbitrage shipments by a third party (usually a wholesaler) taking advantage of differences in prices charged by the originator manufacturer for the same product sold in different countries. Such parallel trade has been explicitly authorized within the European Union (EU) for trade between EU countries but not from outside the EU. In the United States, parallel trade is precluded by traditional patent law. However, current proposals before Congress would permit importation into the United States of drugs produced in a Food and Drug Administration (FDA) approved facility in Canada or several other countries.

12. Manufacturers might achieve a relatively high price in the Netherlands by launching new products first in the unregulated U.K. and German markets, delaying launch in the more tightly regulated markets of France and Belgium. Because the Dutch price ceilings apply throughout the life of the product, they would likely be more binding for older compounds, particularly those with generics available in the benchmark countries.

13. A formal model of the effects of RP and drug budgets is developed in Danzon and Liu (1996).

14. These spillovers apply only to originator products because generics are generally not subject to cross-national price regulation and are rarely parallel traded.

15. Our data from 1998 predate the 1999 downward revision of RP levels based on these capped prices. Following this revision, RPs may be a binding constraint for more products, leading to more clustering at the RP than we observed in our 1998 data.

16. We use the IMS therapeutic classification system, which is similar to the World Health Organization's anatomical therapeutic classification (ATC) system.

17. IMS defines a standard unit as a proxy for a dose for each formulation. For oral forms, a standard unit is one tablet or one capsule; for liquids, it is 5 milliliters, etc. Our dollar price estimates use the average exchange rates, implied by the IMS data, of DM.554 = $1, NLG.492 = $1, and $NZ.557 = $1.

18. Cox proportional hazard model estimates show that the launch hazard for a new compound in New Zealand compared to Germany became significantly lower after 1994 (Danzon and Ketcham 2004 forthcoming).

19. Two additional molecules, sotalol and fenofibrate, were approved in the United States during this time period but were in at least one of the three other countries prior to 1980, so they were excluded from the analysis in table 1.2.

20. The price (RP) relative for each molecule is defined as the ratio of the weighted average price (RP) for the molecule in the comparison country (the Netherlands or New Zealand) relative to that molecule's price (RP) in Germany.

21. The same pattern occurs if molecules are categorized by their global launch date rather than by country-specific launch date.

22. In table 1.4, the RP for each molecule is the volume-weighted average of the pack-level RP per standard unit for all packs in the molecule in each country. The analysis is based on matching molecules, but formulations may differ across countries. The estimates may be biased for the unconditional effects of RP if, for example, more expensive formulations are less likely to be launched in New Zealand for reasons other than RP.

23. The surcharge coefficients are not exactly the difference between the price and RP coefficients because we use the log transformation of price and RP, which are approximately log normal, whereas surcharge is in dollar units because it can be negative.

24. While our proxy for molecule efficacy is its Global age, the regime indicators are based on the Country-specific age.

25. All equations include indicator variables to identify products for which there was imputation of the subsidy because of imperfect matching of our price and subsidy data sets.

26. RP requires the patient to pay 100 percent of the price differential of the new drug compared to the older, cheaper drug, whereas under a fixed percentage co-insurance of, say, 20 percent, the patient would pay only 20 percent of the price differential of the newer drug. Under the typical PBM formulary structure, the patient pays a tiered copayment, say, $5 for a generic, $15 for a preferred brand, and $30 for a nonpreferred brand. Consider a class with three products: a generic, an originator product in molecule A that is off-patent, and an originator product in molecule B that is on-patent. A typical formulary would place off-patent originator A on the nonpreferred tier, and generic A and originator B on the preferred tier. A patient who wants originator A must pay the full originator price differential of brand A relative to generic A. For on-patent originator B, however, the out-of-pocket price to the patient is only $15 and the PBM pays the manufacturer price minus the $15 and minus any discounts negotiated by the manufacturer to get the preferred tier placement.

27. The evidence suggests that price competition among on-patent, therapeutic substitute products is fairly weak in the absence of management by a PBM, possibly because unmanaged drug demand is dominated by physicians, who are not highly price-sensitive. If the Medicare drug benefit uses the proposed 25 percent co-insurance rate, this might induce more price sensitivity in patients and physician-agents and hence more price competition. Still, it seems likely that using a tiered formulary, with its leverage to negotiate discounts on on-patent drugs, would offer seniors a better trade-off between out-of-pocket exposure and choice of drug than would an RP system.

28. Brand-generic price differentials are significantly higher in the United States than in most other countries because the United States has both relatively low generic prices and relative high originator prices (Danzon and Furukawa 2003).

29. External referencing is discussed in Danzon (1997).

References

Danzon, P. M. (1997). "Price Discrimination for Pharmaceuticals: Welfare Effects in the US and the EU," *International Journal of the Economics of Business*, 4:301–321.

Danzon, P. M. (2001). "Reference Pricing: Theory and Evidence," in G. Lopez-Casasnovas and B. Jonsson (eds.), *Reference Pricing and Pharmaceutical Policy*. New York: Springer.

Danzon, P. M., and L. Chao (2000). "Cross-National Price Differences for Pharmaceuticals: How Large, and Why?" *Journal of Health Economics*, 19:159–195.

Danzon, P. M., and M. Furukawa (2003). "Cross-National Price Differences for Pharmaceuticals: Evidence from Nine Countries." Health Affairs.

Danzon, P. M., and J. Ketcham (2004 forthcoming). "The Effects of Reference Pricing on Prices, Availability and Utilization of Pharmaceuticals," The Wharton School, University of Pennsylvania, working paper.

Danzon, P. M., and H. Liu. (1996). "Reference Pricing and Physician Drug Budgets: The German Experience in Controlling Pharmaceutical Expenditures," University of Pennsylvania, working paper.

Danzon, P. M., Y. R. Wang, and L. Wang (2002). "The Impact of Price Regulation on the Launch Delay of New Drugs—Evidence from Twenty-Five Major Markets in the 1990s," *NBER* working paper no. 9874.

de Vos, C. (1996). "The 1996 Pricing and Reimbursement Policy in the Netherlands," *PharmacoEconomics*, 10Suppl2:75–80.

Huskamp, H. A., M. B. Rosenthal, R. G. Frank, and J. P. Newhouse (2000). "The Medicare Prescription Drug Program: How Will the Game Be Played?" *Health Affairs*, 19(2):18–23.

Ioannides-Demos, L. L., J. E. Ibrahim, and J. J. McNeil (2002). "Reference-Based Pricing Schemes: Effect on Pharmaceutical Expenditure, Resource Utilisation and Health Outcomes," *PharmacoEconomics*, 20(9):577–591.

Jonsson, B. (2001). "Reference Pricing: Central Economic Issues," in G. Lopez-Casasnovas and B. Jonsson (eds.), *Reference Pricing and Pharmaceutical Policy*. New York: Springer.

Kanavos, P., and U. Reinhardt (2003). "Reference Pricing For Drugs: Is It Compatible With U.S. Health Care?" *Health Affairs* 22:16–31.

Kletchko, S. L., D. W. Moore, and K. L. Jones (1995). "Targeting Medicines: Rationalising Resources in New Zealand." Wellington, New Zealand: Pharmac.

Lopez-Casasnovas, G., and J. Puig-Junoy (2001). "Review of the Literature on Reference Pricing," in G. Lopez-Casasnovas and B. Jonsson (eds.), *Reference Pricing and Pharmaceutical Policy*. New York: Springer.

Kanavos, P., and U. Reinhardt (2003). "Reference Pricing for Drugs: Is It Compatible with U.S. Health Care?" *Health Affairs*, 22(3):16–30.

Ma, C. T., and M. H. Riordan (2002). "Insurance, Moral Hazard, and Managed Care," *Journal of Economics & Management Strategy* 11(1):81–108.

Maasen, B. M. (1995). *Reimbursement of Medicinal Products: The German Reference Price System. Law, Administrative Practice and Economics*. Zellik, Belgium: Center for New Europe.

Merck Frosst Canada (1996). *Policy Paper on Health Care Cost Containment*. Vancouver, Canada.

Morton, F. S. (1997). "The Strategic Response of Pharmaceutical Firms to the Medicaid Most-Favored-Customer Rules," *Rand Journal of Economics*, 28(2):269–290.

Pauly, M. V. (1968). "The Economics of Moral Hazard: Comment (in Communications)," *The American Economic Review*, 58(3):531–537.

Pavcnik, N. (2002). "Do Pharmaceutical Prices Respond to Patient Out-of-Pocket Expenses?" *Rand Journal of Economics*, 33(autumn):469–487.

Pharma Pricing Review (1996).

Remit Consultants (1991). *Cost Containment in the European Pharmaceutical Market: New Approaches*. London: Remit Consultants.

Rigter, H. (1994). "Recent Public Policies in the Netherlands to Control Pharmaceutical Pricing and Reimbursement," *PharmacoEconomics*, 6(Suppl1):15–24.

Sanders, J. (2001). "Pharmaceutical Reference Pricing," presentation, Advance PCS, ISPOR Conference, May.

Schneeweiss, S., S. B. Soumerai, R. J. McGlynn, M. MacClure, C. Dormuth, and A. M. Walker (2002). "The Impact of Reference-Based Pricing for Angiotensin-Converting Enzyme Converting Inhibitors on Drug Utilization," *Canadian Medical Association Journal*, 166(6):737–745.

Schoffski, O. (1996). "Consequences of Implementing a Drug Budget for Office-Based Physicians in Germany," *PharmacoEconomics*, 10 (Suppl2)81–88.

Thomas, M. C., J. Mann, and S. Williams (1998). "The Impact of Reference Pricing on Clinical Lipid Control," *New Zealand Medical Journal*, 111:292–294.

Ulrich, V., and E. Wille (1996). "Health Care Reform and Expenditure on Drugs," *PharmacoEconomics*, 10 (Suppl2):81–88.

VFA (Verband Forschender Arzneimittelhersteller) (2000). *Statistics2000*. Berlin, Germany: Verband Forschender Arzneimittelhersteller.

Woodfield, A. (2001). "Theory and Evidence from New Zealand," in G. Lopez-Casasnovas and B. Jonsson (eds.)., *Reference Pricing and Pharmaceutical Policy*. New York: Springer.

Zeckhauser, R. J. (1970). "Medical Insurance: A Case Study of the Tradeoff between Risk Spreading and Appropriate Incentives," *Journal of Economic Theory*, 2(1):10–26.

2

Adverse Selection and the Challenges to Stand-Alone Prescription Drug Insurance

Mark V. Pauly, *University of Pennsylvania and NBER*
Yuhui Zeng, *University of Pennsylvania*

Executive Summary

This paper investigates a possible predictor of adverse selection problems in unsubsidized stand-alone prescription drug insurance: the persistence of an individual's high spending over multiple years. Using Medstat claims data and data from the Medicare Survey of Current Beneficiaries, we find that persistence is much higher for outpatient drug expenses than for other categories of medical expenses. We then use these estimates to develop a simple and intuitive model of adverse selection in competitive insurance markets and show that this high relative persistence makes it unlikely that unsubsidized drug insurance can be offered for sale, even with premiums partially risk adjusted, without a probable adverse selection death spiral. We show that this outcome can be avoided if drug coverage is bundled with other coverage, and we briefly discuss the need either for comprehensive coverage or generous subsidies if adverse selection is to be avoided in private and Medicare insurance markets.

I. Introduction

Providing insurance coverage against expenditures for prescription drugs through unsubsidized but sometimes regulated private insurance markets has proved to be difficult. Medigap policies for the elderly provide only limited coverage and are not taken by many of those over 65. Of those not covered by employer-paid plans, only a small fraction of seniors take a Medigap policy that pays anything for drugs. For people under age 65, drug-only coverage is almost unavailable, and some managed-care insurers are putting upper limits on the bundled coverage they do offer. In this paper, we use novel methods applied to claims data to show that adverse selection is an important cause of the absence of or limits to stand-alone drug coverage for both populations.

We also argue that private markets without substantial subsidies will not be able to offer stand-alone drug coverage. This means, we will show, that such coverage is neither to be expected nor desired for the under-65 population; the more integrated coverage that characterizes managed care may therefore be more feasible than a return to the old Blue system in which each type of provider fielded a separate type of insurance. We also show that Medicare policy makers should likewise be cognizant of the chance of adverse selection for stand-alone coverage. If stand-alone coverage is not feasible for the under-65 population, as we show, that analysis also provides evidence that it is also likely (perhaps even more likely) not to be feasible for the over-65 population. Examination of adverse selection in the under-65 market is of interest in its own right, both as a test of the general hypothesis that unsubsidized, unbundled coverage is not feasible and as a warning that such coverage is neither to be encouraged nor expected.

We then go further to develop a method that shows what type of bundling and/or what types and levels of subsidies would be needed to make voluntary drug coverage (public or private) workable. We illustrate these methods with data for both the under-65 and the over-65 (Medicare) populations.

II. Adverse Selection in Concept and Application to Prescription Drugs

A potential threat to the efficiency and even the feasibility of unsubsidized private-market insurance coverage for any expense is adverse selection. Adverse selection occurs when potential insurance buyers are better able to predict their expected benefits from insurance than are insurers, or when insurers are forbidden to charge higher premiums to those they expect to claim higher benefits. Such special buyer knowledge, should it occur, can have many causes, but adverse selection by new health insurance purchasers is surely more likely if there are health conditions known to the buyer for which above-average expenditures will persist over time (Crippen 2002).

If the insurer is not as well informed as is the buyer about the existence of these conditions, or the insurer is not permitted to charge higher premiums to those expected to have higher expenses, a buyer with high and persistent expenditures in one period will be eager to obtain generous insurance coverage of that type of expenditure for the next period at premiums that do not fully reflect the higher expected benefits. Similarly, those with low expected expenses will be less willing to pay insurance premiums that substantially exceed their expected claims.

While insurers may ask applicants about prior-period spending, it will be difficult for them to enforce truthful revelation for prospective purchasers they have not previously insured and for whom they have no prior claims data. Community rating rules may prevent them from gathering or using that information. Because group insurance typically does not vary the premiums with risk across options, and because Medicare itself is likely to use a uniform premium for any drug coverage option, in what follows we usually assume pure community rating. We do, however, inquire whether using adjusted community rating (adjusting premiums for age and gender) would make a difference and find that it would not. In summary, adverse selection in the sale of new coverage is likely to be a more serious problem, other factors being equal, for conditions and medical product expenditures that persist over time than for conditions and product expenses which are unexpected and generally resolve fairly quickly (by patient recovery or death).

Another vehicle used by buyers to engage in adverse selection when consumers can choose among different health plans (in individual or group markets) is an ability to select the details of coverage for various types of expenses. Most generally, it is easier for buyers to engage in adverse selection if they can pick and choose the amounts and types of coverage rather than take or leave a predetermined broadbased policy. If a person knows that he or she had high previous-period medical expenses on certain medical goods or services, adverse selection is enhanced by the ability to choose coverage that only (or primarily) covers these costs.

Thus, we investigated the persistence over time of high levels of spending for a type of medical care that is often a candidate for selective coverage: outpatient prescription drug expense. The problem of adverse selection is thought to be especially acute in individually chosen, unsubsidized, but regulated and partially community-rated Medigap drug coverage. The failure of basic Medicare to cover outpatient drugs has meant that seniors with incomes above the Medicaid limits seeking such coverage must do so largely in the currently unsubsidized private market, either in the form of supplementary Medigap coverage or a managed-care plan with such coverage. For the under-65 population, there is at present much less stand-alone drug coverage than in Medicare (probably for the reasons we identify), but the extent of coverage can vary across the options available to employees in larger firms or to purchasers in the individual market.

Several sources of data exist for prescription drug benefits for both under-65 and over-65 (Medicare) populations. Because we wanted to investigate the effect of combining, or bundling, drug coverage with other coverage, this study required information on a population's use of benefits for all covered medical services as well as for drugs. Because we wanted to examine persistence over a reasonably long period of time, we wanted data that covered multiple years. Therefore we examined two sets of data: (1) a large sample of claims data for drugs *and* other kinds of medical spending for a working-age population and (2) data on Medicare beneficiaries from the Medicare Current Beneficiary Survey (MCBS). We also used a subanalysis of workers in the five years before Medicare eligibility at age 65 to show that the problem of persistence in spending is worse for them than for younger adults because the extent of and prevalence of persistent expenditures increases with age.

The key issue in predicting the extent of adverse selection is the distribution of expected expenses in a population charged a uniform insurance premium. We propose a simple method to estimate this distribution and to use this estimate along with an assumption about the strength of risk aversion to see if adverse selection is likely to emerge.

Our research differs from that presently available in several ways. Some studies examine the persistence of drug spending from one year to the following year only (Ettner 1997; Long 1994; van Vliet 1992; Wouters 1991, Coulson and Stuart 1992), but we follow spending over periods of three to five years. Some studies looked at long-term persistence for total medical-care spending (Eichner et al. 1998), but none explored the category of drug spending. Some studies also looked at adverse selection (and moral hazard) in the Medigap market as a whole (Wolfe and Goddeeris 1991). They used sophisticated (but rather fragile) econometric methods to determine adverse selection and separate it from moral hazard. They also did not look at drug spending and drug coverage specifically. In contrast, we use a different method based on direct estimation of the distribution of risks to judge the likelihood of adverse selection, and we apply that method to drug coverage as well as comprehensive coverage. The recent study by Atherly (2002) is closest to ours because it looks at adverse selection in Medigap drug coverage, but it does not consider more comprehensive drug coverage or stand-alone drug coverage.

III. Methods

First we explore the relative importance of persistence in prescription drug expenditures compared to other expenditures. To show the impact of persistence and selective coverage on adverse selection, we then take the analysis two steps further. In the first step, we simulate the equilibrium premiums in insurance markets for drug coverage alone and for comprehensive (all medical services) coverage. We show that adverse selection under community rating or with some risk rating is much worse in the former case than in the latter, in two senses. First, the ratio of the market equilibrium premium to the premium that would have prevailed if all (risk-averse) people bought coverage is higher for unsubsidized stand-alone drug insurance than for comprehensive coverage: because of the widely skewed distribution of expected expenses, low-risk people would need to pay proportionately much more than their average expenses. Even fairly risk-averse people at the median risk level would be unlikely to pay the premiums that insurers must charge to cover their costs. Second, the risk premium is smaller for stand-alone drug coverage than for comprehensive coverage precisely because drug expenses are so predictable. Indeed, for many plausible values of consumer risk premiums and some plausible assumptions about insurer premium rating, we show that it is impossible to offer stand-alone drug insurance at premiums that will cover its costs: unsubsidized insurance suffers from a death spiral.

In the second step, we illustrate the level of subsidies that would be needed to make stand-alone coverage workable. We then offer some observations on the policy trade-offs, for both Medicare and the private sector, between subsidies and the bundling of coverage.

Our initial analysis is based on claims data provided by the Medstat group for a large sample of workers and adult dependents with comprehensive insurance that covered prescription drugs over a five-year period from 1994 to 1998, inclusive. We use this data set to develop estimates of adverse selection in unsubsidized insurance for the under-65 population; the large size of this database allows us to examine the impact of several variants of the basic model. We then use the validated basic model to analyze adverse selection in the smaller MCBS data set.

The high consistency of results across both data sets reinforces our confidence in the results.

Data and Descriptive Statistics: Medstat Under-65 data

We followed the Medstat claims and benefits expenditure experience of those persons who retained coverage over the entire period. (We also looked at those who were in the database for shorter periods of time, but their experience is not described here.) We do not know the details of each person's coverage, but the plans are known to be similar in terms of coverage. Our results could be biased if people who remained with these plans over a five-year period were those with unusually high drug expenses. However, because the coverage for this population is employment-based and is chosen by and for a group of workers, not an individual worker, and because, as noted, stand-alone drug coverage is not generally available in groups, we think the bias should be small. We did not include data on people who died. But the data still provide valid measures from the viewpoint of the surviving population who might purchase insurance.

Following Eichner et al. (1998), we first describe persistence by asking what happened over time to the (relative) expenditure levels for various categories of expenditures of those who had unusually high expenses in the first period (1994). We characterize high spenders in 1994 in two ways—as being in the top quintile of 1994 expenses and as spending more than $5,000. (Those with zero expenditures are included in the population.)

There were 140,981 persons between the ages of 22 and 64 in 1998 who had continuous medical and pharmacy coverage for the period 1994–1998.[1] As shown in table 2.1, of those in the top quintile of total spending in 1994, only 46 percent remained in that quintile by 1998. The largest decline occurred in the first year, with a more gradual erosion later.

Table 2.1
Percentage of those initially in the highest quintile who remained in the highest quintile after 1994[a]

	1995	1996	1997	1998
Inpatient, outpatient, and drug expenditures	54	50	48	46
Inpatient and outpatient expenditures	47	43	42	40
Drug expenditure only	76	69	63	60

[a]$N = 28{,}146$ (in highest quintile); 100% of sample in highest quintile in 1994.

Table 2.1 also shows the percentages remaining in the top quintile for drug expenditures only and for total expenditures minus drug expenditures. By this measure, persistence is definitely higher for drug expenditures; 60 percent remained in the top drug-spending quintile in 1998, while only 40 percent remained in the top quintile for expenditures other than drugs.

Table 2.2 shows the percentage of those with expenses above $5,000 who also had expenses above that level in the next year, a measure used by Eichner et al. (1998). Persistence tends to rise with age, and our figures are very close to those in the Eichner study.

Next we calculated, for each of the expenditure categories, the ratio of the average expenditure in each year of those who were in the top quintile in 1994 to the average expenditure for the entire population in that year. The higher this number, the more likely is adverse selection. As shown in table 2.3, the ratio between the average or expected expenses of high spenders and the community (average) rate is almost identical in the initial year (1994) for the two categories of spending, but in all subsequent years, it is considerably higher for drug spending only than it is for total spending. This indicates that, in any single time period, drug expenditures display about the same amount of skewedness as other medical expenditures. The major difference is that, in subsequent periods, those with unusually high drug expenses

Table 2.2
Percentage spending more than $5,000 in second year, by age: comparison of results

Age	Our data	Eichner et al. (1998)
0–17	20.59	19.21
18–35	19.46	20.79
36–45	24.14	25.07
46–55	25.78	28.6
56–65	29.64	26.6

Table 2.3
Ratio of top quintile average spending to overall average spending[a]

	1994	1995	1996	1997	1998
Total spending	3.9	2.5	2.3	2.2	2.2
Drug spending	3.9	3.5	3.2	3.0	2.8

[a]$N = 140,981$ (for overall spending); $N = 28,146$ (for highest quintile).

are much more likely to repeat that high spending than are those initially with high spending in other categories. The level of expected drug expenses is much more predictable for an individual than is the level of other expenses.

Potential Adverse Selection in the Medstat Data

To determine the potential seriousness of adverse selection for different types or combinations of types and to determine whether it might be serious enough to cause a death spiral, we used a simulation model. Under the assumption that the person must either buy the indicated coverage or none at all, we assume various levels of risk aversion and estimate what proportion of consumers will continue to buy coverage and what will be the average expense of those willing to buy. For the present, we also ignore moral hazard and assume that the level of expense that insurance will cover is the same as the expense the person who declines coverage would pay out-of-pocket.

We approach this problem in two ways, which we label statistical and economic. In both cases we focus on predicting 1998 expenses. The methods differ in the technique used to estimate the expected expense for each person. In the statistical (or actuarial) approach, people are classified into cells based on age, gender, and prior spending. The cell mean expense in 1997 is used as an estimate of expected expense in 1998; this approach explores persistence only over a two-year period. In the economic approach, in contrast, a regression relating expenses in 1998 to age, gender, and expense in the previous four years is used to generate expected expense in the last year both for drug spending and for spending on other types of inpatient and outpatient medical care.[2]

This expected expense (estimated under either method) compared to actual expense generates an estimate of the variance of expenses, which is combined with an assumed uniform risk-aversion coefficient to generate a value for the risk premium (Phelps 2003). The same approach to estimating the risk premium is used in both the statistical and economics methods; the methods differ in how they generate estimates of the variance in spending for individuals. Note that the more predictable the expense, the lower the variance and therefore the lower the buyer risk premium (and the more likely is adverse selection, other factors being equal). Adding the risk premium to the expected expense yields a reservation price for full insurance coverage for a given type of expense for each person. If the reservation price for a person at a given risk level is less than the insurance premium that would be charged, we assume that the person declines coverage. Allowing the risk-aversion coefficient to vary across individuals for a given value of the variance of spending would not alter the results as long as it is not correlated with expected expense or variance.

The key step then is to determine for a given policy (described by full coverage of the batch of covered expenses: all expenses; all expenses less drug spending; drug spending only) whether there is a stable equilibrium or whether there is a spiral that drives some or all potential insured persons at a given risk level out of the market. That is, we ask what proportion of the initial population would be willing to pay the premium that a hypothetical actuarially fair insurer would have to charge to cover the insurer's own expenses.[3]

We consider full coverage insurance without patient cost sharing and initially ignore moral hazard. We also ignore insurer administrative costs and initially assume that the insurance premium must be strictly community rated but sufficient to cover benefits costs so that the premium charged for a policy offered to a given set of people is the average expected expense for the people in that set. Offering that policy at that premium is then a potential equilibrium if each person in the set has a reservation price for insurance that equals or exceeds the insurance premium. For example, one could begin considering whether the community rated premium is below the reservation price of the people in the lowest percentile of expected expenses in the set. If the reservation price falls short of the premium for some of the lower-risk percentiles, we then delete those persons from the data set, compute the breakeven premium again, and check to see if it is below the reservation price of the lowest risk percentile remaining. Finally, as mentioned above, we assume pure community rating unless explicitly noted otherwise.

A Simple Statistical Model

We wish to illustrate how adverse selection is related to the degree of persistence of spending over time and the relative importance of that influence on expected expense. We begin with a simple benchmark model that gives maximum influence to previous-period spending.

We first classify the 141,000 observations on adults by age and gender into eighteen cells and, within each age-gender cell, by deciles of 1997 spending. Using the population represented by all of the observations that fell in a decile in 1997, we calculate the mean 1998 expense for that population. We then assume, for each decile age-gender cell, that this quantity is the estimate of expected expense for everyone in the cell.[4] (We have also estimated models with disaggregation into unit percentiles with similar results.) That is, we assume that consumers used this realized mean as their estimate of expenses that they expect in 1998. (To the extent that individual consumers use more information than we have assumed, adverse selection will be even worse.) We also assume that the variance of within-cell spending about the cell mean provides an estimate (used by consumers in that cell) of the expected variance of spending for individuals in each cell.

To calculate the risk premium, we must make an assumption about risk aversion. We use various assumed values for the "coefficient of risk aversion" (Phelps 2003). If we use a coefficient of risk aversion of 0.0002, for example, we calculate the risk premium RP according to the formula:

$RP = 0.5 (0.0002)(\text{variance of spending})$

We then define the reservation price P by:[5]

$P = RP + (\text{expected expenses})$

If all persons were expected to purchase insurance, the 1998 competitive (breakeven) community-rated premium would be the mean of 1998 benefits B. (Other administrative costs and insurer profit are ignored here.) That premium would be a competitive equilibrium price only if every person had a higher reservation price than the premium. If that were the case, all would buy insurance, and average expenses for insured persons would turn out to be just covered by the insurer's premium, which equals the population's average expense.

Suppose, however, that P for the lowest risk decile is less than B. All the persons with risk in that decile will decline coverage, and an insurer would anticipate incurring expenses that are the mean of expenses for persons in the other nine deciles, an amount larger than B. We then determine whether P for the second lowest decile is higher or lower than this new mean. If it is not, the premium will have to increase further, and the process continues until we reach a decile at which the value of P for that decile is greater than the mean expense or premium for the remaining population of purchasers. If the only group for which this is true is the highest decile of 1997 expenses, we can say that there has been a death spiral in which all people but those with the highest risks have been driven from the market.

Table 2.4 shows the simulation results from this process. (Note that, because the table shows the result of a simulation, not an estimation, there are no goodness of fit or other statistical measures.) The numbers in the table indicate the decile of spending above which insurance would be purchased in equilibrium for a range of plausible values for risk aversion.[6] For example, if $r = 0.0002$, the equilibrium for total spending occurs in the seventh decile, which means that somewhat more than half of the population (those in deciles 1 to 6) would not buy insurance to cover all medical costs because the premium exceeds their reservation prices, but a sizable minority would be willing to purchase. In contrast, according to this method, the equilibrium premium for drug-only coverage occurs in the tenth (highest) decile, which means that only the people with the very highest risks (if anyone) would buy drug coverage. Altering the assumed degree of risk aversion affects the proportion of the population who would buy comprehensive coverage, but there is no plausible level of risk aversion at which most people buy stand-alone drug coverage.

An Economic Model
The alternative estimation approach begins with a regression of 1998 expenses on a constant term and expenses in the previous four years, controlling (with binary variables) for age and gender. The regression equation is:

$$\text{DRUGEXP}_{it} = \sum_{k=1}^{4} \alpha_{ik}\, \text{DRUGEXP}_{t-k} + \sum_{j}^{n} \text{AGEGENDERDUM}_j$$

where DRUGEXP_{it} is the drug expense of a person i in period t, and AGEGENDERDUM_j is a binary variable for whether the person is in the jth of n different age-gender cells.

We used a linear functional form based on previous work (Pauly and Herring 1999) that showed a linear form to be a good predictor of expected expenses and preliminary analysis of the data that confirmed

Table 2.4
Statistical demand simulation with community rating: lowest decile at which insurance is purchased, by type of coverage and coefficient of risk aversion (CRA)

	CRA = .0001	CRA = .0002	CRA = .0003	CRA = .0009
Total	9th decile	7th decile	5th decile	1st decile
Total – drug	9th decile	5th decile	5th decile	1st decile
Drug only	10th decile	10th decile	10th decile	10th decile

this result for this data. Table 2.5 presents the variables used and some statistics from these regressions. As expected, the adjusted R squared is much higher for the drug-only regression (0.6) compared to the other two regressions (0.19 and 0.13); drug expenses are much more predictable. (Coefficients for the seventeen binary age-gender variables are not shown.) Also, the coefficients on previous-period spending are larger and more precisely estimated for drug-only spending than for the other two measures of spending. While current-period drug spending is largely determined by drug spending in the immediate past period, current-period spending on other types of medical care depends strongly on spending over several years in the recent past.

We next calculate the standard error of the prediction from the regression and use this result as an estimate of the variance of expenses for each individual. For various values of risk aversion, we then calculate the (proportional) risk premium. For example, for total expenses and $r = 0.0001$, the proportional risk premium is 0.745. This result implies that, rather than go without insurance, the person would be willing to pay a premium 1.745 times as high as expected expense (equivalent to a maximum loading as a percentage of premium of

Table 2.5
Regression coefficients and t statistics (dependent variable: spending in 1998)[a]

Adjusted R-squared		Coefficient	t
.6081	Drug 1997	.7788105	252.104
	Drug 1996	.1420874	30.871
	Drug 1995	.0477469	9.038
	Drug 1994	.05911	14.364
.1887	Total 1997	.3428897	116.631
	Total 1996	.134076	40.740
	Total 1995	.1210086	32.510
	Total 1994	.0962468	30.061
.1316	Inpatient and outpatient expenditures 1997	.3010067	102.155
	Inpatient and outpatient expenditures 1996	.111741	34.359
	Inpatient and outpatient expenditures 1995	.0954854	26.032
	Inpatient and outpatient expenditures 1994	.082087	26.149

[a] $N = 140,981$; prob $> F = .0000$ for all three regressions.

43 percent). In contrast, the proportional risk premium for drug-only coverage is much lower, at 0.054. Severe adverse selection occurs in drug-only coverage because of the combination of high predictability of drug spending and consequent low willingness to pay much more than expected expenses.

We apply the same proportional risk premium to each person's expected expenses to generate an estimate of the reservation price. We then arrange individuals in order based on expected expenses and follow the same procedure as in the previous case.

Table 2.6 shows the results in terms of the percentile of the distribution of expected expenses at which people buy coverage under the assumption of pure community rating. The results are striking: despite some adverse selection, comprehensive total coverage can be sold to much of the population if people are moderately risk averse; there will not be a serious spiral. But even at the highest level of risk aversion, very few buy stand-alone drug coverage. With the lowest value of risk aversion ($r = 0.0001$) there is also a fairly severe problem of adverse selection even with more comprehensive coverage. With higher levels of risk aversion, however, spirals do not occur for more comprehensive coverage, and 70 to 99 percent or more of the population would choose in equilibrium to obtain this insurance rather than go without. The proportion of lower risk persons who drop out is, of course, higher if drug expenses are included in the comprehensive coverage than if they are left uncovered.

We investigated what would happen if, instead of pure community rating, insurers were able or were permitted to use a modified system of community rating in which premiums varied by purchaser age and gender (which are easy to determine) but not by prior-period medical-care spending. We assume that premiums are set equal to average benefits in gender–five-year age cells. (Even our large data set does not allow precise estimates of spending for single-year age cells.) Table 2.7

Table 2.6
Economic demand simulation with pure community rating: lowest percentile at which insurance is purchased, by types of coverage and coefficient of risk aversion (CRA)

	CRA = .0001	CRA = .0002	CRA = .0003	CRA = .0009
Total	95th percentile	27th percentile	12th percentile	3rd percentile
Total – drug	83rd percentile	15th percentile	6th percentile	1st percentile
Drug only	99th percentile	99th percentile	99th percentile	98th percentile

Table 2.7
Economic demand simulation with modified community rating: lowest percentile at which insurance is purchased, by type of coverage and coefficient of risk aversion (CRA)

	CRA = .0001	CRA = .0002	CRA = .0003	CRA = .0009
Total	92nd percentile	7th percentile	3rd percentile	1st percentile
Total – drug	55th percentile	4th percentile	1st percentile	1st percentile
Drug only	99th percentile	99th percentile	99th percentile	98th percentile

shows that permitting some risk rating reduces the predicted amount of adverse selection and leads to a larger proportion of the population buying coverage, as one would expect. (In this model, high-risk people never find premiums to be unaffordable because there is no moral hazard and no income effects on the risk premium.) Even with modified community rating, however, stand-alone drug coverage cannot be profitably marketed; there are still spirals under all assumptions about risk aversion.

What happens to these estimates if we add the possibility that the expenses that consumers will pay without insurance may be less than those they pay when they have coverage? That is, what happens if we account for moral hazard, which seems to characterize outpatient drug spending (Newhouse et al. 1993, Hillman et al. 1999)? If some of the expenses paid by insured persons are caused by moral hazard and therefore have values to consumers that are less than their costs, comprehensive insurance coverage will be less attractive than in the no-moral-hazard case (Pauly 1971). More people will decline coverage, and adverse selection will be worse.

We simulate the effect of moral hazard by assuming that 20 percent of insured drug spending is attributable to moral hazard.[7] Under conventional economic assumptions, the value of this additional spending will be half of its cost.[8] The effect of moral hazard therefore is to reduce the total value of drug insurance by 10 percent. As would be expected, the combination of moral hazard and adverse selection reduces the proportion of people estimated to buy comprehensive coverage even further, by about 10 percent. As before, almost no one buys stand-alone drug insurance.

Finally, we specifically examine the Medstat experience of the age group closest to Medicare: those age 55 to 59 in 1994 (who were 60 to 64 at the end of the period). As already noted in table 2.3, the year-to-year correlation of spending is highest in the oldest age group. (The expense prediction regression for this subgroup, which is not shown, is estimated from data for this subgroup only.) Table 2.8 shows that, as before, adverse selection prevents the purchase in market equilibrium of drug-only coverage. Compared to table 2.6, the market share of coverage that bundles drug spending with other medical expenses (total expenses) is smaller for this age group than for the overall population at low values of risk aversion but is higher at higher values of risk aversion.

These simulation-based estimates of the proportion of the population remaining in the market are obviously not definitive, but they do strongly suggest that, for reasonable assumptions about parameter values, it would be very difficult for a market to offer unsubsidized stand-alone drug coverage, even in the under-65 market. Of course, a substantial tax subsidy coupled with the offer of group insurance coverage may make such a policy feasible in the employment-based group insurance market. Even here, problems are likely if stand-alone insurance were offered in a multiple-choice setting. What is most important in this analysis, however, is the comparison of market equilibria between all-inclusive coverage and drug-only coverage. Drug-only coverage causes much more severe adverse selection even if it does not go into a death spiral. Based on these findings, it should then be unsurprising that drug-only coverage is rare among the non-elderly. And in multiple-choice employment settings, it appears to be relatively rare for an employer to offer a choice among plans that do and do not offer drug coverage. While offerings vary in other dimensions, employers tend to choose either all plans with drug benefits, or no plans with drug benefits.

Medicare Drug Spending
We assembled a three-year panel (1997–1999) of Medicare beneficiaries from the MCBS. Persons with incomes so low they were on or were

Table 2.8
Economic demand simulation for persons age 60–64 with no moral hazard and pure community rating: lowest percentile at which insurance is purchased, by type of coverage and coefficient of risk aversion[a] (CRA)

	CRA = .0001	CRA = .0002	CRA = .0003	CRA = .0009
Total	99th percentile	70th percentile	1st percentile	1st percentile
Total – drug	99th percentile	1st percentile	1st percentile	1st percentile
Drug only	99th percentile	99th percentile	99th percentile	98th percentile

[a]$N = 14,478$.

eligible for Medicaid were excluded; the Medicare population we study is the one that might be expected to be potential purchasers of voluntary insurance. The number of observations is 2,945 in each year. We regressed 1999 spending for each person on spending in the prior two years along with additional binary variables (age and gender). (Regression results are available from the authors.) As before, the explanatory power of spending in prior periods is much greater for drug spending than for total spending ($\bar{R}^2 = 0.34$ for drug spending and 0.18 for total spending), and there is a statistically significant effect of spending in prior years on total spending.

We then used the coefficients and statistics from this regression to determine the probable extent of adverse selection. Using the same methods as we did earlier, we show in table 2.9 that stand-alone drug spending is generally not feasible for the Medicare population, even at breakeven premiums. Bundled coverage could induce voluntary purchasing, however, if risk aversion is moderate.

Needed Medicare Subsidy
Ignoring moral hazard and the possibility of risk rating, we estimated the subsidy to stand-alone drug coverage that would be needed to get 80 percent of the Medicare population to buy such coverage voluntarily if their only other alternative was no coverage. (This calculation does not account for the availability of coverage through Medicaid or employer programs; it is intended to be illustrative of the orders of magnitude involved.) We do this by setting the subsidy equal to the difference between the willingness to pay of the group at the 80th percentile and the breakeven premium for the 80 percent of the population with the highest risk. Table 2.10 shows that the estimated subsidy is large as a percentage of the premium for this group. Adding the administrative loading costs would doubtless raise the absolute and relative subsidies needed.

Table 2.9
Economic demand simulation with pure community rating for the medicare population: lowest percentile at which insurance is purchased by type of coverage and coefficient of risk aversion (CRA)

	CRA = .0001	CRA = .0002	CRA = .0003	CRA = .0009
Total	89th percentile	1st percentile	1st percentile	1st percentile
Drug only	99th percentile	99th percentile	99th percentile	64th percentile

Table 2.10
Estimated subsidy necessary to induce 80 percent of the Medicare sample to purchase comprehensive stand-alone prescription drug coverage, by coefficient of risk aversion (CRA)

	Subsidy for 80% purchase	
CRA	Dollar amount	Percentage of premium
.0001	908	91
.0002	883	89
.0003	857	86
.0009	704	71

IV. Conclusion

This analysis leads us to suspect strongly that drug-only coverage cannot be sold in competitive insurance markets at premiums that cover its cost. Even for middle-class people, its sale would require a substantial subsidy.

These results are also germane to discussions of publicly funded reinsurance of large medical expenses that provoke adverse selection (and intrusive underwriting screening to avoid adverse selection) in private insurance (Swartz 2002). The results imply that this problem is likely to be especially severe for drug expenses, even more so than for larger expenses associated with other types of medical care that display less persistence over time. One might therefore conclude that reinsurance that would provide the most appropriate incentives and relief to insurers would take into account *both* the amount and the persistence of large claims.

Another main result is that all-inclusive insurance policies will be less subject to adverse selection than drug-only coverage for the same population. Having said this, however, we cannot conclude that unregulated competitive markets will necessarily be able to furnish such coverage. People in the lowest ranks of expected drug spending could have higher expected utility from coverage that excludes drugs than from coverage that includes it. That is, coverage that excludes drugs may drive out all-inclusive coverage (that, of course, includes drugs). As long as it is permitted to sell such coverage, and ignoring other economies or jointness advantages of comprehensive coverage, we conclude that coverage excluding drugs would tend to drive out coverage that includes drugs. It is instructive, however, that even in unregulated under-65 markets, the phenomenon of coverage excluding drugs is now rather rare. In any case, unsubsidized drug-only coverage that would supplement a policy that covers other expenses would barely survive, even if cost offsets are assumed to be zero.

Can insurers incorporate devices into their policies to mitigate the effects of adverse selection? One simple solution would be to limit the frequency with which people are permitted to change coverage, but it is difficult to lock people at low risk into policies with such provisions. Another, more useful method is to incorporate guaranteed renewability at nondiscriminatory premiums as a required policy provision. This device, if properly used, can retain the people with low risk in the pool and greatly diminish the opportunities for adverse selection (Pauly 2003, Herring and Pauly 2003).

Current discussions of drug coverage for the Medicare population often envision stand-alone but fairly generously subsidized community-rated coverage for much of the population. The adverse selection we have identified will be a challenge that must be taken into account, but one that those subsidies (in the short run) and integrated coverage (in the long run) may help to overcome.[9] Our results suggest, however, that the subsidy will need to be generous indeed. One long-term policy choice is between generous subsidies to stand-alone coverage and less heavily subsidized but more carefully designed comprehensive insurance. Another policy choice (for a given public budget) is between a heavily subsidized policy with high deductibles and low adverse selection and more generous coverage with more beneficiary payment of premiums but more adverse selection. How much subsidy is needed and how much redesign would help are issues that should definitely be investigated further.

Notes

Supported by a grant from The Merck Company Foundation. The authors thank Medstat, and especially William Marder, for assistance with this data. The views expressed here are those of the authors and not necessarily those of The Merck Company Foundation or of MEDSTAT, Inc.

1. Since the youngest members of this cohort were 18 in 1994, the total number of persons represents all adult workers and dependents who remained under age 65 in the period.

2. The statistical approach takes into account any differences across cells in the extent to which persistence might itself vary with age or gender. The simple regression model in the economic approach does not allow for such interaction effects, based on preliminary

analysis that found them to be small. Note that this approach assumes that people use only their prior spending to predict their expenses in the next period. If they have additional information (e.g., "I know that this will be the year I plan to get my sore knee fixed but insurers do not"), adverse selection will be worse than what is estimated here.

3. We therefore use only the Medstat claims data and estimate breakeven premiums based on the claims data. We do not use direct measures of premiums actually paid for coverage of those claims.

4. We assume that both insurers and people who are insured have the same average estimate. Some cells are small so that the observed sample mean might not be a precise estimate of the population mean for people with those characteristics, but that imprecision will apply only to a small fraction of the total population.

5. For an explanation of this method, see Phelps (2003), Chapter 10 and especially Appendix A.

6. Phelps (2003) labels 0.0003 a moderately high value of risk aversion, but Pauly and Herring (2000) found it necessary to use a higher level (0.00095) to generate realistic results in a simulation of adverse selection for comprehensive group insurance. A level of 0.0003 would imply that a person in Phelps's example would be willing to buy insurance as long as a premium were no more than 26 percent greater than expected benefits.

7. This value is chosen to be consistent with the −0.2 demand elasticity reported by the RAND Health Insurance Experiment. See Keeler et al. (1988).

8. The assumptions here are that the demand curve is approximately linear over the relevant range and that there are no important income effects on the demand for medical care.

9. One offset is that the greater predictability of drug spending should make it easier in principle to risk-adjust payments to insurers. The insurer used by someone with high current-period expenses will receive a larger payment than the insurer used by someone with low current-period incentives. This diminishes insurer incentives to cream skim, but it does not diminish the incentive to the high spender to choose the more generous plan.

References

Atherly, A. (2002). "The Effect of Medicare Supplemental Insurance on Medicare Expenditures," *International Journal of Health Care Finance and Economics* 2(2):137–162.

Coulson, N. E., and B. A. Stuart (1992). "Persistence in the Use of Pharmaceuticals by the Elderly: Evidence from Annual Claims," *Journal of Health Economics* 11(3):315–328.

Crippen, D. L. (2002). "Projections of Medicare and Prescription Drug Spending, Statement of Dan L. Crippen before the United States Senate Committee on Finance, March 7, 2002." Washington, D.C.: Congressional Budget Office.

Eichner, M. J., M. B. McClellan, and D. A. Wise (1998). "Insurance or Self-Insurance? Variation, Persistence, and Individual Health Accounts," in D. A. Wise (ed.), *Inquiries in the Economics of Aging*, NBER Project Report Series. Chicago, Ill.: University of Chicago Press, 19–45.

Ettner, S. (1997). "Adverse Selection and the Purchase of Medigap Insurance by the Elderly," *Journal of Health Economics* 16(5):543–563.

Herring, B. J., and M. V. Pauly (2003). "Incentive-Compatible Guaranteed Renewable Health Insurance Premiums," *NBER* working paper no. 9888.

Hillman, A. L., M. V. Pauly, J. J. Escarce, K. Ripley, M. Gaynor, J. Clouse, and R. Ross (1999). "Financial Incentives and Drug Spending in Managed Care," *Health Affairs* 18(2):189–200.

Keeler, E. B., J. Buchanan, J. E. Rolph, J. M. Hanley, and D. Reboussin (1988). *The Demand for Episodes of Medical Treatment in the Health Insurance Experiment.* Santa Monica, Calif.: RAND.

Long, S. (1994). "Prescription Drugs and the Elderly: Issues and Options," *Health Affairs* 13(2,Part II):157–174.

Newhouse, J. P., and the Insurance Experiment Team (1993). *Free for All? Lessons from the RAND Health Insurance Experiment.* Cambridge, Mass.: Harvard University Press.

Pauly, M. V. (1971). *Medical Care at Public Expense.* Westport, Conn.: Praeger Publishers, Inc.

Pauly, M. V. (2003). "Time, Risk, Precommitment, and Adverse Selection in Competitive Insurance Markets," paper presented at the CESifo Summer Institute, Venice, Italy, July.

Pauly, M. V., and B. J. Herring (1999). *Pooling Health Insurance Risks.* Washington, D.C.: AEI Press.

Pauly, M. V., and B. J. Herring (2000). "An Efficient Employer Strategy for Dealing with Adverse Selection in Multiple-Plan Offerings: An MSA Example," *Journal of Health Economics* 19(4):513–528.

Phelps, Charles E. (2003). *Health Economics,* 3d ed. Reading, Mass.: Addison-Wesley.

Swartz, K. (2002). "Government As Reinsurer for Very-High-Cost Persons in Nongroup Health Insurance Markets," *Health Affairs Web Exclusive* 23 October. Available at http://www.healthaffairs.org/WebExclusives/Swartz_Perspective_Web_Excl_102302. htm (access date October 31, 2002).

van Vliet, R. C. J. A. (1992). "Predictability of Individual Health Care Expenditures," *Journal of Risk and Insurance* 59(3):443–460.

Wolfe, J. R., and J. H. Goddeeris (1991). "Adverse Selection, Moral Hazard, and Wealth Effects in the Medigap Insurance Market," *Journal of Health Economics* 10(4):433–459.

Wouters, A. V. (1991). "Disaggregated Annual Health Services Expenditures: Their Predictability and Role as Predictors," *Health Services Research* 26(2):247–272.

3

Disability Forecasts and Future Medicare Costs

Jayanta Bhattacharya, *Stanford University and NBER*
David M. Cutler, *Harvard University and NBER*
Dana P. Goldman, *RAND and NBER*
Michael D. Hurd, *RAND and NBER*
Geoffrey F. Joyce, *RAND*
Darius N. Lakdawalla, *RAND and NBER*
Constantijn W. A. Panis, *RAND*
Baoping Shang, *RAND*

Executive Summary

The traditional focus of disability research has been on the elderly, with good reason. Chronic disability is much more prevalent among the elderly, and it has a more direct impact on the demand for medical care. It is also important to understand trends in disability among the young, however, particularly if these trends diverge from those among the elderly. These trends could have serious implications for future health care spending because more disability at younger ages almost certainly translates into more disability among tomorrow's elderly, and disability is a key predictor of health care spending.

Using data from the Medicare Current Beneficiary Survey (MCBS) and the National Health Interview Study (NHIS), we forecast that per-capita Medicare costs will decline for the next fifteen to twenty years, in accordance with recent projections of declining disability among the elderly. By 2020, however, the trend reverses. Per-capita costs begin to rise due to growth in disability among the younger elderly. Total costs may well remain relatively flat until 2010 and then begin to rise because per-capita costs will cease to decline rapidly enough to offset the influx of new elderly people. Overall, cost forecasts for the elderly that incorporate information about disability among today's younger generations yield more pessimistic scenarios than those based solely on elderly data sets, and this information should be incorporated into official Medicare forecasts.

I. Introduction

To help the government take the actions necessary to keep Medicare solvent, the Center for Medicare and Medicaid Services (CMS) needs to generate accurate predictions for future health care spending. This requires predicting how many people of various types will be alive in each future year and what their health care spending will be.

The first part of this exercise is to project population size. Official projections of the aged beneficiary population by age and gender are available from prominent sources such as the Social Security Administration (SSA). These projections already account for the long-run trends in decreasing age-specific mortality rates. The SSA population estimates make it clear that the baby boomers will swell the ranks of the elderly significantly starting in 2010. Forecasting per-capita health expenditures for people of a given age is a more difficult proposition. Individual health care spending is influenced by many factors: age, gender, health status, diseases and the medical technology to treat them, the price of care, insurance coverage, living arrangements, and care from family and friends. Spending estimates are uncertain because it is difficult to predict changes in these factors and in their relationships to health spending. One can assume, as most actuarial models do, that health care spending remains constant within a given age-gender category. In that case, estimated future Medicare expenditures are influenced only by changes in the age composition of the population and general trends in spending that are applied uniformly across age-gender categories. This approach overlooks several key factors, however, including the importance of changes in disability and health status among the future elderly.

Disability has been shown in numerous contexts to be an important predictor of elderly health care costs. For example, Goldman et al. (2003) find that elderly with multiple activity limitations can have up to ten times higher mean Medicare costs than those with no limitations, and similar patterns occur in median spending. One possibility is that disability simply reflects a different disease, but even within chronic diseases, they find that elderly with greater disability can have up to three times higher spending. Clearly Medicare forecasts will be highly sensitive to disability trends.

In this paper, we present a natural and straightforward method for forecasting elderly disability from observed disability among the young. The principal forecasting problem, is that trends in disability among the young have not been stable or consistent. Overall, disability among the young has been increasing somewhat, but the rate of increase has varied substantially. For example, the early 1990s saw the sharpest and most dramatic increases in disability among the young, while the late 1980s and mid 1990s saw more muted growth. These different rates of increase have completely different implications for future health care expenditures.

II. Methods

Data

We use information from the National Health Interview Survey (NHIS) and the Medicare Current Beneficiary Survey (MCBS) to predict disability and the MCBS to predict costs. The NHIS is a nationally representative set of individual-level data on demographics and health status and is designed to represent the noninstitutionalized population. It has been collected every year since 1957. The stability of the NHIS survey design makes it particularly attractive for analyzing long-run trends in disability. Although the survey was redesigned in 1982 and 1997, it is possible to construct consistent estimates from 1984 to 1996. The MCBS is a nationally representative sample of the Medicare population. Because nearly all permanent U.S. residents over age 65 are eligible for Medicare, we can use this population segment as a sample of the over-65 population. The MCBS has the advantage of including the institutionalized population as well as the noninstitutionalized. We use the NHIS to measure disability for people under age 65 but the MCBS to measure disability for people over age 65. Below, we describe a procedure for producing a complete age-profile of disability by reconciling the disability estimates across the two data sets.

The MCBS is a nationally representative data set designed to ascertain utilization and expenditures for the Medicare population, especially those expenditures borne by the beneficiary or supplemental insurance. The sample frame consists of aged and disabled beneficiaries enrolled in Medicare Part A and/or Part B, although we use only the aged. The MCBS attempts to interview each person twelve times over three years, regardless of whether he or she resides in the community, resides in a facility, or moves between community and facility settings. The disabled (under 65 years of age) and the oldest old (85 years of age or over) are oversampled. The first round of interviewing was conducted in 1991. Originally, the survey was a longitudinal sample with periodic supplements and indefinite periods of participation. In 1996, the MCBS switched to a rotating panel design with limited periods of participation. Each fall, a new panel is introduced, with a target sample size of 12,000 respondents, and each summer a panel is retired. The MCBS contains detailed self-reported information, including the prevalence of various conditions, measures of physical limitation in performing activities of daily living (ADLs) and instrumental activities of daily living (IADLs), and height and weight. In addition, the MCBS contains detailed self-reported data on health service use, as well as Medicare service use records. Institutionalized respondents are interviewed by proxy. To measure disability, we use the ADL questions in the MCBS. Specifically, respondents are asked whether they have any difficulty with bathing or showering, dressing, eating, getting in or out of chairs, walking, and using the toilet. Therefore, an individual in the MCBS can have anywhere from zero to six ADLs.

The NHIS can be used to measure disability among those under age 65 according to a similar measure, but the ADL questions are not asked in the NHIS until 1995. This feature is troublesome because we wish to project trends in future health in part by examining long-run trends in past disability. The NHIS *does* ask earlier questions about disability from 1982 onward. In the 1995 NHIS, respondents are asked both the ADL questions and the earlier disability questions. This feature will allow us to link the earlier disability measures with the ADL measures and thus construct measures of ADL limitations going back to 1982.

From 1982 to 1995, the NHIS began asking all respondents over age 60, as well as all those age 5 to 59 who reported some activity limitation, if they needed help with personal care.[1] Based on a respondent's answer to the personal care question, she or he was placed in one of three categories: (1) unable to tend to personal care needs, (2) limited in performing other routine needs, (3) not limited in personal care or routine needs. In a 1995 disability supplement, the NHIS asked both these personal care questions as well as another set more similar to the MCBS questions. The NHIS reports whether individuals have any difficulty with bathing or showering, dressing, eating, getting in and out of bed or chairs, walking, or using the toilet. These questions are more similar to the MCBS, but they were asked only in 1995. To construct estimates for earlier years, we use the 1995 data to construct a map from the personal care variables to the number of ADLs. This is done using an ordered probit regression where the dependent variable is the number of ADLs, and the independent variables are dummy variables for an individual's personal care needs, age, gender, and race.

The result of this procedure is a single, combined data set representative of the entire population age 25 and over.[2] Each person in the sample is assigned several ADLs, along with other reported demographic characteristics. We characterize the disability of every individual in the sample by placing her or him in one of three mutually exclusive disability states: institutionalized, having zero ADL limitations, or having at least one ADL. All individuals in the latter two categories are noninstitutionalized. Defining nursing home residence as a disability state allows us to use the 1997 and 1998 years of the MCBS, during which disability among the institutionalized is measured differently. Because the NHIS represents our only data source for people under age 65, and because it is confined to the noninstitutionalized, we are forced to assume a zero rate of institutionalization for people under 65.

The rates of disability by age group are shown in table 3.1. A sharp break in reported disability occurs at age 65, when we switch from the NHIS data to the MCBS data. In general, reported rates of disability are much lower in the NHIS than those in the MCBS. Some of this difference can be attributed to different wording in survey questions, but rates are lower in the NHIS even for identically worded questions. This issue is discussed in more detail in Goldman et al. (2003). We propose a method for dealing with this discrepancy in the following section.

Forecasting Disability

To forecast disability, we first construct smooth age-prevalence profiles of disability from the 1992–1996 data sets. The smoothing procedure is

Table 3.1
Prevalence of disability by age group[a]

Age group	Zero ADLs	Some ADLs	Nursing home
25–29	99.72	0.28	—
30–34	99.56	0.44	—
35–39	99.4	0.6	—
40–44	99.29	0.71	—
45–49	99.17	0.83	—
50–54	98.95	1.05	—
55–59	98.6	1.4	—
60–64	97.81	2.19	—
65–69	79.75	18.74	1.51
70–74	76.43	21.31	2.26
75–79	67.22	28.22	4.57
80–84	54.53	34.74	10.73
85–89	37.99	39.82	22.19
90+	19.66	40.67	39.66

[a]Figures for people younger than 65 are based on 1992–1996 NHIS. Figures for people older than 65 are based on 1992–1996 MCBS. Figures for the elderly should not be compared to the figures for people younger than 65 for reasons discussed in the paper.

described in the appendix. We perform smoothing separately for the population under age 65 in the NHIS and then for the population over age 65 in the MCBS.[3] The NHIS and MCBS results are based on different questionnaires, so we do not simply combine the two prevalence profiles. Instead, we take the MCBS prevalence profile as the measure of disability for people over age 65. To construct the profile for the under-65 population, we combine estimates of disability *incidence* from the NHIS with the MCBS prevalence for people who are 65. For example, to calculate the prevalence of disability among 64-year-olds, we take the MCBS prevalence among 65-year-olds and then subtract the incident cases of disability for people between the ages of 64 and 65 in the NHIS. In this manner, we extrapolate backward in age, back to age 25. This method yields a full age-prevalence profile that is, broadly speaking, comparable to the levels in the MCBS measurement scheme.

Using these age-prevalence profiles, we calculate the extent to which aging raises the prevalence of disability (in more formal language, we compute age-incidence profiles). This approach allows us to age the 1996 population forward through the life cycle and construct forecasts of disability in the future. Suppose, for example, that the prevalence of disability rose by an average of 2 percentage points between the ages of 65 and 66, and suppose that 65-year-olds in 1996 exhibited a 10 percent prevalence of disability. We would thus forecast that 66-year-olds in 1997 would exhibit a 12 percent prevalence of disability. This approach allows us to compute the forecasted prevalence of disability at any age and future year t. Call this prevalence of disability $d(t, a)$. To forecast the number of disabled people at each age and year, we use population projections. The Census Bureau projects population for single-year age categories for every year until 2100. This yields estimates of $p(t, a)$, the population of people age a in year t. The number of disabled people age a in year t is thus $D(t, a) = p(t, a) * d(t, a)$. For simplicity, we treat population growth and disability trends as being independent of each other.

Forecasting Costs
Given estimates of the disabled population, we need a way to translate disability into health expenditure forecasts. We do this in the context of linear regression. The primary dependent variables used in the cost regressions are Medicare reimbursements and their components (Part A and Part B reimbursements) and total medical expenditures. We use longitudinal data from the Medicare Current Beneficiary

Survey (MCBS) cost and use files (1992–1998) to estimate average Medicare expenditures for persons age 65 to 90, conditional on their health status. We regress monthly Medicare reimbursements for each individual in the sample on disability status (i.e., which of the three disability states an individual is in), linear age splines, and health/age interactions separately for males and females. The coefficients from these models are used to predict monthly Medicare expenditures for each age/gender/health cell. As in the disability forecasts, we use the MCBS respondents over age 65, but for the purposes of estimating cost, we also exclude people enrolled in health maintenance organizations (HMOs) and those without Part B supplemental Medicare insurance, because of incomplete ascertainment of health care utilization. These exclusions yield an average yearly sample of about 9,400 beneficiaries.

Given our cost regressions, we can translate the forecasted size of the disabled population in every year into projected health expenditures. We first compute from the expenditure equation the average health care expenditures for individuals who are age a and of disability status k. We call this $e(k, a)$. Assuming the real price of health care is rising with general inflation—an assumption that admittedly understates true price growth (Chernew, Hirth, and Cutler 2003)—total health care expenditures in year are then given by:

$$\sum_{a=25}^{\infty} \sum_{k=1}^{3} e(k, a) * D(t, a; k)$$

III.   Results

Forecasts of Disability

The resulting forecasts of disability are shown in figures 3.1 through 3.4. The figures show forecasted prevalence of disability for four different age groups. Figure 3.1 tells the story: while the rate of institutionalization does not change, the prevalence of disability among those in the community is predicted to fall until 2015 but then to stabilize and even rise slightly thereafter. The figures make clear that the reversal of disability trends comes from the young cohorts entering old age—in figure 3.2, disability does not decline at any time for individuals age 65 to 74. Disability stops falling in figure 3.3 for 75- to 84-year-olds around 2010, while it does not do so until nearly 2020 for those over age 85 in figure 3.4. Indeed, the growth in disability is not all that substantial for this oldest age group.

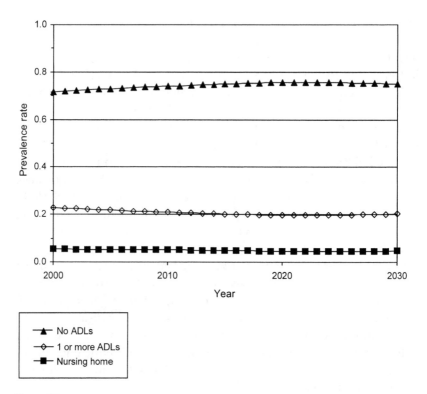

Figure 3.1
Forecasted prevalence of disability among people age 65 or older

We performed the following check on our disability forecasts. We used NHIS data from the 1980s to forecast disability growth for the population under age 65 from 1990 to 1996.[4] We then compared these forecasts to actual disability rates in the 1990s. Figure 3.5 displays the results. It is significant that our method understates actual growth in disability over time. The forecast error shifts down as we move from 1990 to 1996. Therefore, our predictions for cost growth should be viewed as perhaps a lower bound on actual cost growth.

Disability and Health Care Costs
Cost profiles by age and health state are shown in Figures 3.6 and 3.7 for males and females, respectively. Medicare beneficiaries age 65 and older who experience difficulty in walking, dressing, or getting out of bed have substantially higher medical expenditures than those without limitations. Among the noninstitutionalized, for example, persons

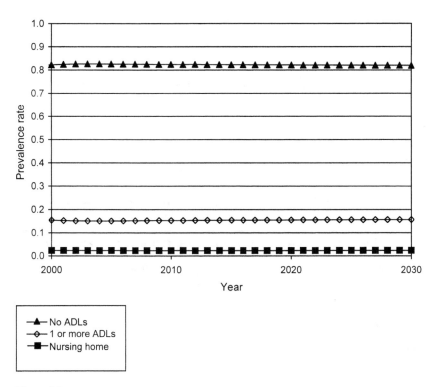

Figure 3.2
Forecasted prevalence of disability among people age 65 to 74

reporting one or more ADLs incur roughly $500 more in monthly Medicare expenses than similar-age adults without limitations. Although compositional changes are likely to confound cost profiles, the impact of age on medical expenditures is best observed by examining the costs of healthy beneficiaries (noninstitutionalized, no ADLs). Monthly Medicare costs increase monotonically among the healthy, rising by $50 to $100 per ten years of life.

The most salient difference across health states is higher monthly expenditures for males. Noninstitutionalized women without ADLs have 25 to 50 percent lower monthly expenditures than similar-age males, and the gap widens in absolute terms as health status worsens. Clear gender differences also exist in the cost profiles of nursing home residents. Average monthly Medicare costs among institutionalized women rise rapidly from age 65 to 70 and then decline consistently for a decade before leveling off. In contrast, average Medicare costs peak

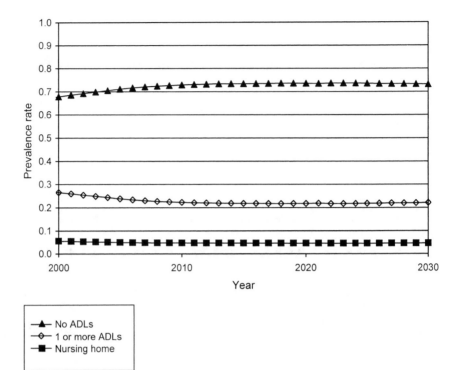

Figure 3.3
Forecasted disability rates among people age 75 to 84

around age 75 for institutionalized males and remain near that level thereafter.

Forecasting Health Expenditures

We combine the age-gender-disability profiles of Medicare costs from the previous section with our forecasts of population in each age-gender-disability cell to produce forecasts of Medicare costs. This results in forecasts of costs that are in terms of blended 1992–1998 dollars; the weights across years are governed by the MCBS sampling scheme. Figure 3.8 displays our forecast of per-capita Medicare costs by age group, while figure 3.9 displays forecasted total costs by age group. Figure 3.8 bears out our disability forecasts by showing a slight projected increase in per-capita costs for people age 65 to 74 but declines for those above age 75. Perhaps more striking is the narrowing of the gap between the per-capita

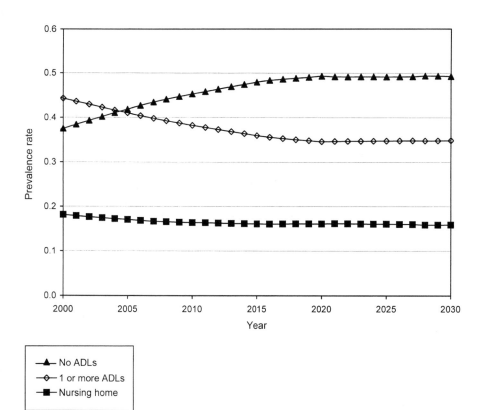

Figure 3.4
Forecasted disability rates among people age 85 or older

costs of 65 to 74-year-olds and the per-capita costs of the entire over-65 population. From the start of our forecast period, there is a steady and substantial narrowing of the age gap in per-capita Medicare costs. Total costs look a bit different largely because population growth among the oldest old is projected to be more rapid than among the young old. The important implication of figure 3.9 has less to do with age effects and more to do with timing. Total Medicare costs are projected to be quite flat for the next several years, in spite of population growth, but they begin a steady ascent shortly thereafter. The growth in per-capita costs that we project causes accelerating growth in total costs after 2015. In other words, the future path of Medicare costs is unlikely to resemble its current path mostly because trends in disability may reverse themselves.

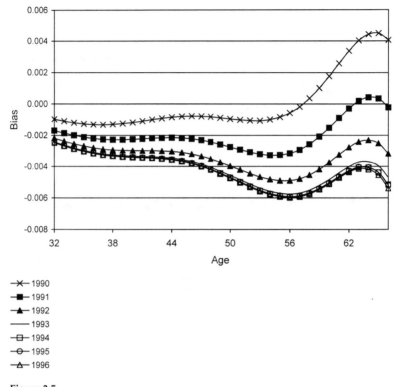

Figure 3.5
Forecast error in NHIS, 1990–1996

The effect of disability on forecasted costs can be seen most clearly if we calculate the implications for costs of different disability scenarios. Figure 3.10 depicts our forecasts for per-capita costs along with the forecasts that would result from three other scenarios: constant disability prevalence, disability declines at the rate experienced from 1989 to 1994 as calculated by Manton et al. (1997) using the National Long Term Care Survey (NLTCS), and disability declines at the rate observed in the NLTCS from 1994 to 1999 (Manton and Gu 2001). Table 3.2 summarizes the differences.

First, it is useful to understand future costs in the context of constant disability. Only the age and gender structure of the population changes under this scenario. Aging is expected to reduce per-capita costs somewhat between 2005 and 2020 with the influx of the young old who will accompany the aging of the baby-boom cohort. By 2020, however, the continued aging of the baby boomers will start to raise per-capita costs.

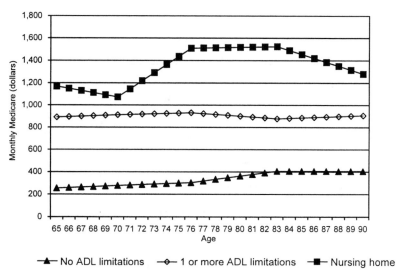

Figure 3.6
Monthly Medicare reimbursement by age and health state for males

Table 3.2

Scenario	Description
Base	Age-prevalence profile changes based on trends in the MCBS (for the elderly population) and the NHIS (for people younger than 65).
Constant	Age-prevalence profile fixed based on initial year. For the entering cohort of 65-year-olds, disability is projected using NHIS prevalence and trend data.
Manton et al (1997)	Age-prevalence profile changes based on trends in NLTCS from 1989–1994 (including the entering cohort of 65-year-olds).
Manton and Gu (2001)	Age-prevalence profile changes based on trends in NLTCS from 1994–1999 (including the entering cohort of 65-year-olds).

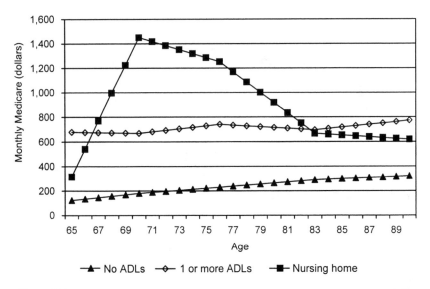

Figure 3.7
Monthly Medicare reimbursement by age and health state for females

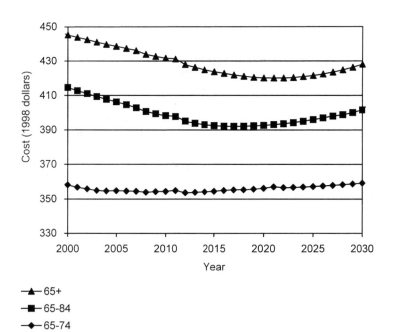

Figure 3.8
Forecasts of per-capita monthly Medicare costs by age group

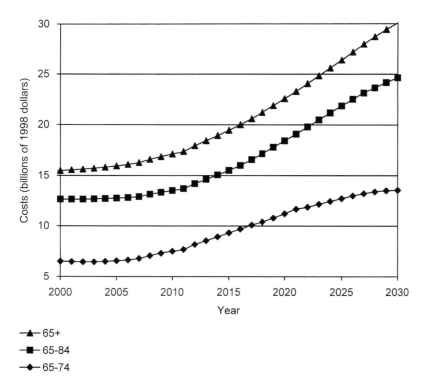

Figure 3.9
Forecasts of total monthly Medicare costs by age group

The constant disability curve makes clear, however, that the vast majority of the projected decline in per-capita costs owes itself to future declines in disability. The extent and duration of these declines are then crucial in governing the path of per-capita costs. Three scenarios are possible for disability change shown on the graph: our scenario, one assuming constant rates of decline in disability equal to the decline between 1989 and 1994, and one assuming constant rates in disability equal to the decline between 1994 and 1999. At the start of the forecast period in 2000, our model actually produces the most optimistic forecasts for per-capita costs. However, the rate of decline from 2000 onward is much slower than in either of the other two scenarios for disability decline. Just after 2010, per-capita costs in our scenario overtake per-capita costs for the disability decline scenarios. Indeed, by 2018, we forecast that per-capita costs will cease to decline and begin to rise. From 2010 onward, our scenario actually tracks the constant disability

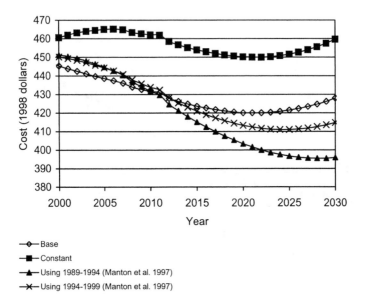

Figure 3.10
Impact of disability forecasts on per-capita Medicare costs
Notes: This figure shows projections of per-capita Medicare costs under four scenarios as described
in the text. The base case is our projection incorporating information on disability trends from the
NHIS (for the young) and the MCBS (for the elderly). The constant case assumes fixed age-prevalence
profiles for disability. The other two cases assume changes in the elderly age-prevalence profile based
on trends observed in the National Long Term Care Survey and ignore NHIS trends among the
young.

case. By 2030, our model predicts real monthly Medicare costs that are
$2 billion higher (in 1998 dollars) than those implied by the disability
declines measured between 1989 and 1994, and $1 billion higher than
those implied by the declines between 1994 and 1999.

IV. Conclusions

Disability is not just a feature of old age. Economic development and
technological change in health care have allowed people *at all ages* to
live in frailty with greater ease than at any other time in history. Any
analysis of disability must account for changes in disability among the
young as well as the elderly. From the mid-1980s to the mid-1990s, the
young have reported an increase in disability, even as the old have
become relatively healthier. Forecasts based on trends in the disability
among the old tend to overstate the benefit of these changes.[5]

Our forecasts imply that per-capita Medicare costs will decline for the next fifteen to twenty years; this finding is in accordance with recent declines in disability among the elderly. By 2020, however, per-capita costs begin to rise as a result of growth in disability among the young old. As these young-old cohorts age, per-capita costs will continue to grow. Total costs may well remain relatively flat until 2010 and then begin to rise as per-capita costs will cease to decline rapidly enough to offset the influx of new elderly people. As a result of growth in per-capita costs, total costs will then begin to grow at an accelerating rate.

Appendix 3.1

Forecasting the disabled population is straightforward once we have constructed smooth age-prevalence profiles of disability. We cannot do so simply by averaging disability within single-year age categories. Even in large, nationally representative data sets, this results in very noisy profiles. To address this problem, we rely on the idea that disability prevalence should change smoothly across ages and years. Therefore, we take the raw age-specific estimates of disability and smooth them across ages and years using an overlapping polynomial method.[6]

Each observation i, taken in $year_i$, consists of information about i's self-reports regarding disability limitations δ_i and age (age_i).[7] As discussed earlier, an individual can be in one of three mutually exclusive disability states: institutionalized, no ADLs, or at least one ADL. Therefore, δ_i can take on one of three values, and so we need to construct age-prevalence profiles for all three levels of disability: $d(t, a; 1), \ldots, d(t, a; 3)$. To begin this process, we estimate the following multinomial logit model of disability using the combined NHIS/MCBS data from 1992 through 1996:

$$\pi\left(\delta_i = 1 \middle| a_i, t\right) = \frac{1}{1 + \sum_{d=1}^{3} \exp\left(g_1(a_i)\beta_1^d + g_2(t)\beta_2^d\right)}$$

$$\pi\left(\delta_i = 2 \middle| a_i, t\right) = \frac{\exp\left(g_1(a_i)\beta_1^2 + g_2(t)\beta_2^2\right)}{1 + \sum_{d=1}^{3} \exp\left(g_1(a_i)\beta_1^d + g_2(t)\beta_2^d\right)} \qquad (3.1)$$

$$\pi\left(\delta_i = 3 \middle| a_i, t\right) = \frac{\exp\left(g_1(a_i)\beta_1^3 + g_2(t)\beta_2^3\right)}{1 + \sum_{d=1}^{3} \exp\left(g_1(a_i)\beta_1^d + g_2(t)\beta_2^d\right)}$$

In effect, we calculate the prevalence of disability at each age and year in the context of a logistic distribution. The g functions allow the presence of disability to vary with the year of observation and the age-cohort of the respondent. Age and year enter the model through the functions, which are specified using an overlap polynomial.

The age polynomials are defined as:

$$g_1(age_i) = \sum_{j=0}^{K} \left[\Phi\left(\frac{age_i - k_{j+1}}{\sigma_1}\right) - \Phi\left(\frac{age_i - k_j}{\sigma_1}\right) \right] p_j(age_i; \beta_{1j}). \tag{3.2}$$

where $p_j (age_i; \beta_{1j})$ $j = 0, \ldots, K + 1$ are all n^{th}-order polynomials in age_i.[8] The terms $k_0 \ldots k_{k+1}$ are called knots, and σ_1 is a smoothing parameter; all are fixed before estimation. With this smoothing technique, the knots define age intervals. When the smoothing parameter approaches zero, the age-profile over each interval simply equals the average disability level within that interval. In this case, the age-profile reduces to a step function, where each interval constitutes a separate step.[9] As the smoothing parameter increases, the estimator uses increasingly more information from outside each interval. In the extreme, as the smoothing parameter approaches infinity, there is no meaningful distinction between any two intervals. Allowing nonzero values of the smoothing parameters eliminates the sharp discontinuity of the growth rates at the knots. One advantage of overlapping polynomials over traditional splines is that the function and all its derivatives are automatically continuous at the knots without imposing any parameter restrictions.

The overlapping polynomials for year, g_2, and its interaction with g_1 allow for flexible changes in the age-prevalence relationship over time. They are defined as:

$$g_2(year_i) = \sum_{j=0}^{M} \left[\Phi\left(\frac{year_i - m_{j+1}}{\sigma_2}\right) - \Phi\left(\frac{year_i - m_j}{\sigma_2}\right) \right] q_j(year_i; \beta_{2j}) \tag{3.3}$$

As before, the m terms represent the knots, while the σ term represents the smoothing parameter.

The object of the maximum likelihood logit estimation is to obtain consistent estimates for β_1, β_2 and $\beta_3 - \hat\beta_1$, $\hat\beta_2$ and $\hat\beta_3$ respectively. Using these estimates, generating age-prevalence profiles representative for any particular year is a straightforward process. Let $d(t, a)$ be the disability prevalence among a-year-olds in year t. Then for $k = 1, 2, 3$:

$$d(t, a; k) = \frac{1}{N} \sum_i \Phi\left[d_i = k \middle| age_i = a, year_i = t; \hat\beta_1, \hat\beta_2, \hat\beta_3 \right] \tag{3.4}$$

We use this expression to construct smooth disability prevalence profiles for the years 1992 to 1996. These are then used in turn as the basis for forecasting changes in disability according to the method discussed in the text.

Notes

This research was supported by the Health Care Financing Administration Centers for Medicare and Medicaid Services and the National Institute on Aging. The views expressed herein are solely those of the authors.

1. The presence of an activity limitation is identified by responses to another set of questions in which individuals are asked to name their major activity and then are asked if they are limited in their performance of that activity. Those who are limited are then asked the personal care question.

2. The sampling weights are adjusted accordingly.

3. For those age 65, we use the NHIS estimates rather than the MCBS estimates; 65-year-olds in the MCBS report artificially high rates of disability due to the sample design. The population under age 65 is disabled by definition because they are eligible for Medicare. Therefore, 65-year-olds include disabled 64-year-olds who age into the over-65 population. The sample is not refreshed quickly enough to eliminate this distortion.

4. We used the 1995 NHIS disability supplement to map the NHIS disability variables into ADL measures. Because no one in the NHIS is institutionalized, we then forecasted the prevalence of 1 + ADLs in the community among the under-65 population.

5. See Manton and Gu (2001).

6. MaCurdy, Green, and Paarsch (1990) were the first to use this method in economics. Bhattacharya, Garber, and MaCurdy (1997) use this method to smooth cause-specific mortality profiles for the elderly.

7. The discussion assumes that d_i refers to disability, but this method was also used for other diseases.

8. We use first-degree polynomials. Although we experimented with higher-order polynomials, we find that they add to the costs of computation with no change in the final results.

9. When this is the case, I (.) reduces to an indicator function equal to 0 if $age < k_j$ and 1 if $age \geq k_j$.

References

Bhattacharya, Jay, Alan Garber, and Thomas MaCurdy (1996). "Cause-Specific Mortality Among Medicare Enrollees," NBER working paper no. 5409.

Chernew, Michael, Richard Hirth, and David Cutler (2003). "Increased Spending on Health Care: How Much Can We Afford?" *Health Affairs*, 22(4):15–25.

Goldman, Dana, Michael Hurd, Paul Shekelle, Sydne Newberry, Constantijn Panis, Baoping Shang, Jayanta Bhattacharya, Geoffrey Joyce, Darius Lakdawalla (2004). "Health Status and Medical Treatment of the Future Elderly: Final Report," RAND Working paper.

MaCurdy, Thomas, David Green, and Harry J. Paarsch (1990). "Assessing Empirical Approaches for Analyzing Taxes and Labor Supply," *Journal of Human Resources*, 25(3): 415–490.

Manton, Kenneth G., Larry Corder, and Eric Stallard (1997). "Chronic Disability Trends in Elderly United States Populations: 1982–1994," *Proceedings of the National Academy of Science*, 94:2593–2598.

Manton, Kenneth G., and XiLiang Gu (2001). "Changes in the Prevalence of Chronic Disability in the United States Black and Nonblack Population Above Age 65 from 1982 to 1999," *Proceedings of the National Academy of Science*, published May 8.

4

Benefit Plan Design and Prescription Drug Utilization Among Asthmatics: Do Patient Copayments Matter?

William H. Crown, *Medstat*
Ernst R. Berndt, *MIT Sloan School and NBER*
Onur Baser, *Medstat*
Stan N. Finkelstein, *MIT Sloan School*
Whitney P. Witt, *Northwestern University*
Jonathan Maguire, *Medstat*
Kenan E. Haver, *Massachusetts General Hospital*

Executive Summary

The ratio of controller-to-reliever medication use has been proposed as a measure of treatment quality for asthma patients. In this study we examine the effects of plan-level mean out-of-pocket asthma medication patient copayments and other features of benefit plan design on the use of controller medications alone, controller and reliever medications (combination therapy), and reliever medications alone. The 1995–2000 MarketScan™ claims data were used to construct plan-level out-of-pocket copayment and physician/practice prescriber preference variables for asthma medications. Separate multinomial logit models were estimated for patients in fee-for-service (FFS) and non-FFS plans relating benefit plan design features, physician/practice prescribing preferences, patient demographics, patient comorbidities, and county-level income variables to patient-level asthma treatment patterns. We find that the controller-to-reliever ratio rose steadily over 1995–2000, along with out-of-pocket payments for asthma medications, which rose more for controllers than for relievers. After controlling for other variables, however, plan-level mean out-of-pocket copayments were not found to have a statistically significant influence on patient-level asthma treatment patterns. On the other hand, physician/practice prescribing patterns strongly influenced patient-level treatment patterns. There is no strong statistical evidence that higher levels of out-of-pocket copayments for prescription drugs influence asthma treatment patterns. However, physician/practice prescribing preferences influence patient treatment.

I. Introduction

It has long been known that trade-offs exist between the gains from pooling across individuals to insure against catastrophic medical expenditures and the efficiency losses from the moral hazard effects that arise because of the implicit marginal subsidies to health services utilization occuring under conventional medical insurance plans.[1] The existence of this trade-off suggests that, given preferences and costs, there may be an optimal amount of coinsurance. Using data from the RAND Health Insurance Experiment in the 1980s, Manning and Marquis (1996) have estimated that, with an $8,000 cap on total expenditures, the optimal coinsurance rate would have been about 50 percent.[2]

Although coinsurance rates for office visits, emergency room visits, inpatient hospitalization, and prescription drug services were set equal in the design of the RAND Health Insurance Experiment, current practice in the United States means that coinsurance and, more commonly, patient copayment amounts differ considerably among the different categories of health care services.[3]

Within the last decade, considerable controversy has arisen involving the design of prescription drug benefits in health insurance plans. This controversy partly reflects the fact that prescription drugs have become an increasingly important component of health care costs, rising sharply from 5.6 percent in 1980 to 9.7 percent in 2000.[4] Continuing a recent pattern, in 2001 total prescription drug expenditures in the United States increased by about 17 percent to $154.5 billion.[5]

Managed-care organizations and the employers with whom they contract have attempted to control rising prescription drug costs by changing cost-sharing provisions, seeking to steer use to preferred drugs on the insurer's list of approved medications (formularies).[6] Already in the early and mid-1990s, plans began experimenting with two-tier copayment schemes in which a low patient copay (say, $5) was assessed for a generic (first-tier) drug, and a somewhat higher but still modest copay (say, $10) was assessed for branded (second-tier) drugs; in some rare cases, physicians needed prior authorization from the payer before being granted permission to prescribe particularly costly medications.

After continued increases in prescription drug costs, in the mid- and late 1990s some plans began implementing less generous three-tier copay schemes. A typical three-tier plan design of several years ago consisted of a $5 copay for a first-tier generic drug, a $10 copay for a preferred branded drug within a given therapeutic class (the second tier); and a heftier $25 copay for the nonpreferred branded (third-tier) drugs within the therapeutic class. Many plans also had a second, more generous three-tier system for mail-order pharmacy prescriptions.

Use of the three-tier copayment designs created incentives not only for insurees to shift toward increased use of the less costly medications, but it also gave insurance plans and payers increased bargaining power with pharmaceutical companies by allowing them to threaten to banish their branded products to the third tier unless drug manufacturers offered the payer substantial discounts or rebates.[7]

Frustrated again by continued increases in prescription drug spending, many plans have recently increased the levels of prescription drug copayments at all three tiers, with the third-tier copayment as high as $40 or $50 per prescription; other plans have turned to the use of coinsurance rather than copayment designs. According to one source, in 2000 the average patient retail copayment for a generic first-tier drug was $7.17; for preferred brands in the second tier, it was $14.14; and for all other nonpreferred brands on the third tier, it was $27.35.[8]

The increased use of multi-tier copayment design mechanisms for prescription drugs raises at least two sets of important issues. (1) Do variations in copay structures alter the level and composition of prescription drug utilization? Are they effective instruments in controlling prescription drug costs?[9] Or do persistent physician prescribing patterns dominate, with copayment variations having only a negligible impact? (2) To the extent three-tier copays affect the level and composition of drug utilization, what are the associated health outcomes? Can copayment design mechanisms be used not only to control costs but also to steer utilization to more medically appropriate uses of prescription drugs?[10]

In this paper, we examine the first set of questions in detail; although we discuss possibilities concerning the second set, we leave it largely for future research. We also examine variation over time and among plans involving copayments for other medical services, such as physician office visits, emergency room treatments, and inpatient hospitalizations.

We address these issues using the therapeutic class of asthma medications as a case study. As described in detail below, asthma drugs can be envisioned as being primarily reliever medications (used to relieve symptoms in an acute asthmatic exacerbation—an asthma attack) or as being primarily controller medications (used to control pulmonary inflammation and prevent an attack). For some time now, health care officials have argued that the appropriate use of controller medications can result in reduced outpatient office visits, emergency room treatments, and inpatient hospitalizations.[11] While the optimal ratio of asthma controller to reliever drug utilization is difficult to quantify precisely (and likely is patient idiosyncratic), it is widely believed that in most cases increases in the controller-to-reliever ratio are beneficial in terms of both economic and medical considerations.[12] A recent historical overview of trends in asthma pharmacotherapy between 1978 and 2002 by Stafford et al. (2002) suggests that, particularly in the last decade, the controller-to-reliever ratio has increased while the number of asthma-related office visits has stabilized or declined.

Before proceeding with a discussion of hypotheses to be tested, underlying data, and econometric methods, we first digress and provide some medical background on asthma and its treatment.

II.   Background on Asthma and Its Treatment

Asthma is a chronic disease characterized by inflammation of the airways and constricted bronchial tubes. Asthma affects about 6 percent of the population and is the third most common chronic condition among children. Although death from asthma is fairly unusual, morbidity from the condition is common. Since 1991, when consensus guidelines on the treatment of asthma were first released by the National Asthma Education Program (1991), clinicians have encouraged the use of maintenance therapy, typically using inhaled corticosteriods to control inflammation and to reverse chronic airway obstruction and hyperreactivity. Other medications, particularly the short-acting beta-two agonist class of bronchodilators, are recommended as reserves for relief of acute episodes of bronchospasm.[13]

Several published articles have examined the benefits that have accrued as the preference of controller over reliever medications for asthma maintenance therapy has gained acceptance.[14] Some of these articles have attempted to correlate a particular metric, commonly called the C/B ratio (the ratio of inhaled corticosteroids to bronchodilators) with populationwide changes in survival and medical services utilization.[15] Greater use of inhaled corticosteroids relative to bronchodilators has been reported to be associated with lower mortality rates and less frequent use of emergency room, inpatient, and outpatient services in the care of patients with asthma.[16]

III.   Hypothesis to Be Tested/Assessed Empirically

We empirically assess the effects of several benefit plan design features on asthma treatment patterns. In particular, we test the hypothesis that higher controller/reliever copay ratios will be associated with reduced use of controller medications, other factors being equal, and whether any effects differ by plan type: fee-for-service (FFS) versus non-FFS plans. Finally, we examine whether physician/practice prescribing patterns influence patient-level asthma treatment patterns and, if so, whether these effects differ between FFS and non-FFS plans.

IV. Data Sources and Construction of Variables

The MarketScan™ private insurance database for 1995–2000 was used in this study. MarketScan™ is the largest database of its kind and contains detailed descriptions of inpatient, outpatient medical, and outpatient prescription drug services for approximately 3 million persons in 2000 who were covered by corporate-sponsored health care plans. These individuals' health care was provided under various fee-for-service (FFS), fully capitated, and partially capitated health plans, including exclusive provider organizations, preferred provider organizations, point-of-service plans, indemnity plans, and health maintenance organizations.

Race, ethnicity, and income information were extracted from a different data set: the Bureau of Health Professions Area Resource File (ARF), a compendium of county-level information produced annually. The ARF data were then merged with the Medstat analytic file by county.

Identification of Asthma Patients
Patients with evidence of asthma were selected from the intersection of the medical claims and encounter records, enrollment files, and pharmaceutical data files. Evidence of asthma was provided by searching the claims data during 1995–2000 for individuals meeting at least one of the following criteria:

• At least two outpatient claims with primary or secondary diagnoses of asthma.
• At least one emergency room claim with primary diagnosis of asthma, and a drug transaction for an asthma drug ninety days prior or seven days following the emergency room claim.
• At least one inpatient claim with a primary diagnosis of asthma.
• A secondary diagnosis of asthma and a primary diagnosis of respiratory infection in an outpatient or inpatient claim.

• At least one drug transaction for a(n) anti-inflammatory agent, oral anti-leukotrienes, long-acting bronchodilators, or inhaled or oral short-acting beta-agonists.

Patients with a diagnosis of chronic obstructive pulmonary disease (COPD) and who had one or more diagnosis or procedure codes indicating pregnancy or delivery or who were not continuously enrolled for twenty-four months were excluded from our study group.

Measures
Sociodemographic Characteristics. The sociodemographic characteristics included the age of the head of the household, percentage of patients who were female, geographic region (Northeast, North Central, South, West, and unknown), member type, and year of entry into the study. In addition, several sociodemographic variables defined at the county level were merged with the patient-level data. These variables included racial composition (percentage of white, black, and other) and income strata.

Plan Type. Fee-for-service plans were defined as plans that did not have an incentive for patients to use a particular list of providers and included basic, major medical, and comprehensive health insurance coverage. The remaining plans, called non-FFS, were defined as plans that either required patients to choose from a list of providers or provided financial incentives to use a specific list of providers. Non-FFS plans included exclusive provider organizations, health maintenance organizations, noncapitated point-of-service plans, preferred provider organizations, or capitated or partially capitated point-of-service plans.

Copayments. Copayments for outpatient pharmaceuticals were calculated by first stratifying all prescription drug claims by year, then by plan within year. Next, we calculated the average out-of-pocket patient copayments for asthma drugs by therapeutic class for each plan, as well as the ratio of mean controller copayments to mean reliever copayments. These plan-level ratios were then attached to each patient's record within a given plan.

We also constructed variables for the average out-of-pocket copayments paid for outpatient physician visits, emergency room visits, and hospital stays. The average copayment captured the actual dollar amount that the patients paid out-of-pocket. Note that we use the term *copayment* to refer to any out-of-pocket payment by individuals for health care. This includes both traditional copayments (e.g., $5 per office visit) as well as coinsurance (e.g., patient pays 20 percent of the bill).

Comorbidities. Several asthma-related comorbidities, including allergic rhinitis, anxiety, depression, gastroesophageal reflux disease (GERD), and migraine, were examined. The number of unique three-digit ICD-9 codes (International Classification of Diseases, Ninth Revision) was used as a proxy for the extent of overall medical and mental health comorbidities.

Charlson Index scores were generated to capture the level and burden of comorbidity. This index draws on diagnostic information from ICD-9 codes and procedure codes, resulting in nineteen conditions that are weighted based on the adjusted risk of one-year mortality. The index score is the sum of the weights for all of a patient's conditions and ranges from one to six, with higher numbers indicating increased levels of comorbidity.[17] The Charlson Index has been highly effective in predicting clinical outcomes and costs.[18] A recent study by Sin and Tu (2001) found that high levels of comorbidity, as measured by the Charlson Index, were strongly associated with the underuse of inhaled steroid therapy in elderly patients with asthma, a finding that is of particular importance for our research.

Utilization. Utilization of health care services or prescription drugs was captured through claims and encounters over the study period. For individuals, we examined the mean annualized number of emergency room visits, hospitalizations, hospital days, outpatient visits, and allergy/asthma specialist visits. Prescription drugs for the treatment of persons with asthma were categorized as either controller or reliever medications. Controllers included inhaled anti-inflammatory agents, oral corticosteroids, oral anti-leukotrienes, and long-acting bronchodilators; relievers were defined as drugs categorized as anticholinergics or inhaled short-acting beta-agonists. Based on this dichotomy, a ratio of controller to relievers was constructed and interpreted as a measure of adequate management of asthma.

Costs. The analytic file contains patients with fee-for-service health plans and those with partially or fully capitated plans. Data on costs were not available, however, for the capitated plans. Therefore, the value of patients' service utilization under the capitated plan was priced and imputed using average payments from the MarketScan™ FFS inpatient and outpatient services by region, year, and procedure.

V. Econometric Methods

Our econometric analysis proceeds in two steps, using a variant of the Lee (1983) multinomial logit selection model, as proposed by Bourguignon, Fournier, and Gurgand (2001). First we model choice among three alternative drug treatments: controller only, reliever only, and a combination of controller and reliever, all on an annual basis. We employ as identifying instruments (variables affecting choice of drug treatment but not total expenditures) plan copayment variables, and physician/provider prescribing composition. Then we employ least squares regressions of log total expenditures for each treatment arm, in addition to a usual set of covariates, the three lambda selection terms (conditional expectations of residuals from the three arms of the treatment selection model).

More specifically, to reduce the potential for endogeneity between plan-level copayment variables and plan-level controller-to-reliever ratios in the multivariate analyses, we utilize a discrete counterpart to the plan-level controller-to-reliever ratio examined in the descriptive analyses. In particular, we construct an annual patient-level dependent variable with three mutually exclusive categories: a controller drug alone (n = 3,903), a combination of a controller drug and a reliever drug (n = 11,427), and a reliever drug alone (n = 11,049). A likelihood ratio test was carried out to examine whether separate models were required for the FFS and non-FFS samples. Based on the results of this test, we estimated separate multinomial logit models for the FFS and non-FFS subsamples. County-level income variables were appended to patient records to augment the medical claims. Robust standard errors were used to adjust for potential intracounty covariance among patients living in the same counties that may have been introduced by these variables. Hausman tests were then conducted to compare selectivity-corrected models with standard ordinary least squares (OLS) models.

In terms of instruments, we construct two sets of identifying variables. Our first set is plan copayments. For each year and plan, we calculate mean copayment values for each class of drug and then take the ratio of controller mean to reliever mean copayment. This plan-specific variable is utilized as a regressor in the multinomial drug treatment choice equations for each person year. A second set involves calculating, for each physician/provider tax identification number in the claims data, the proportion of patients obtaining controller-only, reliever-only, and combination treatment. In many cases this taxation identification number covers a multiphysician medical practice, but in some cases it is unique to one physician. Because the sum of these three percentages is 100 percent for each physician/provider practice, we delete one of the three percentages but include two of them as regressors in the multinomial drug treatment model. We recognize that this approach still leaves room for some selectivity in the form of patients' choice of physician and choice of plan, but we believe nonetheless that this method provides a reasonable first step in mitigating the effects of such selectivity. We also note that, in this paper, we do not examine the implications of treatment patterns on components of subsequent health care utilization, although we do model total health care expenditures.

VI. Descriptive Results

Based on the definitions of asthma episodes discussed above, we obtained a sample that included 44,926 patients in FFS plans and 18, 305 in non-FFS plans (63,231 patients total).

Controller-to-Reliever Ratio
As shown in figure 4.1, the controller-to-reliever ratio has been rising over time. Between 1995 and 1999, it increased by approximately 40 percent, with more rapid increases in the two most recent years. The ratio is consistently higher for patients in FFS plans than for those in non-FFS plans and, since 1997, the rate of increase appears to be higher for the FFS plan beneficiaries than for those in non-FFS plans. Irrespective of plan type, however, almost all plans had average controller-to-reliever ratios greater than 1 (plan-specific data not shown).

Patient Demographics
Table 4.1 reports the demographic characteristics of the sample, stratified by FFS and non-FFS plans. Patients in FFS plans had a mean age of 34 years compared to 27 years for non-FFS plans ($p < .001$) and were more likely to be female (57 percent versus 52 percent, $p < .001$). Patients in FFS plans were also more likely than patients in non-FFS plans to be located in the North Central region (67 percent versus 9 percent,

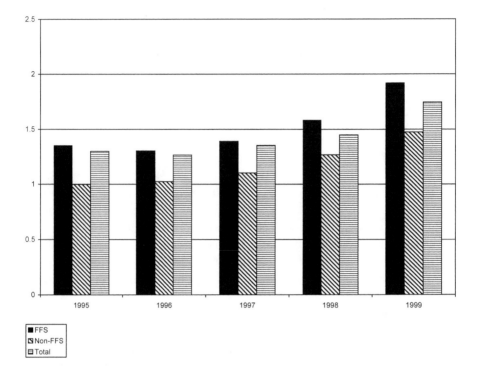

Figure 4.1
Controller/reliever medication ratios by plan type and year

Table 4.1
Summary of asthma patient characteristics by insurance plan type, 1995–2000

	FFS	Non-FFS	Total	p
N	44,926	18,305	63,231	NA
Trigger type				
(1) 2 OP asthma claims	37.05%	36.91%	37.01%	0.74
(2) Asthma ER + asthma RX	0.69%	0.82%	0.73%	0.06
(3) IP resp. inf. + asthma	0.04%	0.08%	0.05%	0.12
(4) IP asthma	0.26%	0.32%	0.28%	0.15
(5) 2 asthma RX	61.97%	61.87%	61.94%	0.82
Mean age	34.09	27.19	32.09	<.01
% females	57.41%	52.09%	55.87%	<.01

Table 4.1
(continued)

	FFS	Non-FFS	Total	p
N	44,926	18,305	63,231	NA
Geographic region				
Northeast	15.63%	47.56%	24.88%	<.01
North central	67.01%	8.76%	50.15%	<.01
South	12.05%	32.76%	18.04%	<.01
West	5.31%	10.92%	6.93%	<.01
Year of trigger				
1996	34.67%	13.13%	28.43%	<.01
1997	20.21%	13.55%	18.28%	<.01
1998	21.99%	14.62%	19.86%	<.01
1999	23.13%	58.71%	33.43%	<.01
Member type				
Employee	40.76%	38.68%	40.16%	<.01
Spouse	22.02%	17.55%	20.73%	<.01
Dependents	37.21%	43.77%	39.11%	<.01
4–11 years	15.76%	27.97%	19.30%	<.01
12–18 years	15.94%	14.24%	15.45%	<.01
Other	5.51%	1.57%	4.37%	<.01
County race/ethnicity				
White				
0–25%	0.49%	0.84%	0.59%	<.01
26–50%	1.44%	7.00%	3.05%	<.01
51–75%	21.25%	35.73%	25.44%	<.01
76–100%	76.82%	56.43%	70.92%	<.01
Black				<.01
0–25%	91.70%	76.30%	87.24%	<.01
26–50%	8.02%	22.85%	12.31%	<.01
51–75%	0.26%	0.85%	0.43%	<.01
76–100%	0.01%	0.00%	0.01%	0.15
Hispanic				
0–25%	96.76%	93.35%	95.77%	<.01
26–50%	2.67%	5.52%	3.49%	<.01
51–75%	0.52%	1.13%	0.69%	<.01
76–100%	0.06%	0.01%	0.04%	<.01
Other				<.01
0–25%	99.94%	99.83%	99.91%	<.01
26–50%	0.02%	0.15%	0.06%	<.01
51–75%	0.04%	0.02%	0.03%	0.21
76–100%	0.01%	0.00%	0.01%	0.20
County mean household income	27,001	31,223	28,269	<.01

$p < .001$) and were more likely to receive their health care coverage as the employee rather than as the spouse or dependent (41 percent versus 37 percent, $p < .001$).

County Race and Income

Substantial differences in racial distribution and mean income between FFS and non-FFS plans were evident from county-level U.S. census data linked to the claims data. The mean household county income of patients covered by FFS plans ($27,001) was significantly lower than that for patients covered by non-FFS plans ($31,223) ($p < .001$). The racial distribution in counties for patients covered by FFS plans was less likely to be white than that of non-FFS plans.

Health Status

As expected given possibilities for adverse selection, patients in FFS plans appear to be sicker than those in non-FFS plans. Table 4.2 documents that patients in FFS plans have higher numbers of major diagnostic categories; higher Charlson comorbidity scores; and higher rates of comorbidities of allergic rhinitis, depression, gastrointestinal disorders, and migraine ($p < .001$ for all comparisons). The rate of comorbid anxiety was not statistically different between FFS and non-FFS plans ($p = 0.78$). Qualitatively similar patterns were evident both for patients age 4 to 11 and those age 12 to 64, although differences were typically larger for adults than for children.

Copayments

Table 4.3 indicates that prescription drug copayments are significantly higher in non-FFS plans than in FFS plans for both asthma medications and nonasthma medications. Across all drugs and all years (1995–2000), the average out-of-pocket copayment made by patients in non-FFS plans was $8.64 compared to $5.20 in FFS plans ($p < .001$). As shown in figure 4.2, however, average controller/reliever copayment ratios were higher in FFS plans than in non-FFS plans, even as FFS plan beneficiaries had greater controller/reliever medication utilization ratios (see figure 4.1). In both types of plans, the controller/reliever copayment ratio has been rising over time along with the increased use of controller medications.

The mean copayments reported in table 4.3 mask considerable variation in copayments over time and across plans. Figure 4.3 illustrates that out-of-pocket copayments for asthma medications have

Table 4.2
Comorbidities among asthma patients by insurance plan type, 1995–2000

	FFS	Non-FFS	Total	p
All patients, N	44,926	18,305	63,231	NA
Number of major diagnostic categories	6.26	5.35	6.00	<.01
Charlson comorbidity index	0.79	0.62	0.74	<.01
Asthma-specific comorbidites				
Allergic rhinitis	23.27%	18.67%	21.94%	<.01
Anxiety	2.39%	2.35%	2.38%	0.78
Depression	10.31%	8.17%	9.69%	<.01
GI disorders	24.55%	20.73%	23.45%	<.01
Migraine	6.02%	5.05%	5.74%	<.01
Patients age 4–11, N	7,084	5,123	12,207	NA
Number of major diagnostic categories	5.19	4.85	5.05	<.01
Charlson comorbidity index	0.55	0.51	0.53	<.01
Asthma-specific comorbidites				
Allergic rhinitis	25.72%	20.69%	23.61%	<.01
Anxiety	0.78%	0.49%	0.66%	0.05
Depression	4.29%	2.81%	3.67%	<.01
GI disorders	15.30%	14.50%	14.97%	0.22
Migraine	3.08%	3.10%	3.09%	0.93
Patients Age 12–64, N	37,842	13,182	51,024	NA
Number of major diagnostic categories	6.46	5.55	6.22	<.01
Charlson comorbidity index	0.84	0.66	0.79	<.01
Asthma-specific comorbidites				
Allergic rhinitis	22.81%	17.88%	21.53%	<.01
Anxiety	2.69%	3.07%	2.79%	0.02
Depression	11.44%	10.26%	11.13%	<.01
GI disorders	26.28%	23.15%	25.47%	<.01
Migraine	6.57%	5.81%	6.38%	<.01

been consistently higher for patients in non-FFS plans compared to patients in FFS plans. Although patients in both types of plans experienced significant jumps in out-of-pocket copayments beginning in 1998, the gap between FFS and non-FFS plans appears to have narrowed. In addition to these time trends, there is high variation in copayment levels for specific drugs within a year. For example, 1999 copayments for fluticasone, an inhaled corticosteroid (a controller medication), varied from $2 in one plan to $28 in another. Similarly, 1999 copayments for albuterol, a short-acting beta-agonist (a reliever

Table 4.3
Plan-level average copayments by insurance plan type, 1995–2000

	FFS	Non-FFS	Total	p
N^a	33,828	18,214	52,042	NA
Prescription copayment	5.20	8.64	6.20	<.01
For asthma-related drugs	5.06	8.04	5.92	<.01
For non-asthma-related drugs	5.24	8.83	6.28	<.01
Outpatient visit copayment	7.71	8.10	7.84	<.01
For asthma-related visits	7.83	8.25	7.97	<.01
For non-asthma-related visits	7.69	8.09	7.83	<.01
Emergency room visit copayment	10.24	13.03	11.22	<.01
For asthma-related visits	15.25	13.92	14.79	<.01
For non-asthma-related visits	9.89	12.94	10.96	<.01
Inpatient visit copayment	16.12	2.78	11.45	<.01
For asthma-related visits	18.07	1.79	12.37	<.01
For non-asthma-related visits	15.92	2.94	11.38	<.01

[a]Average copayment was not available for all plans.

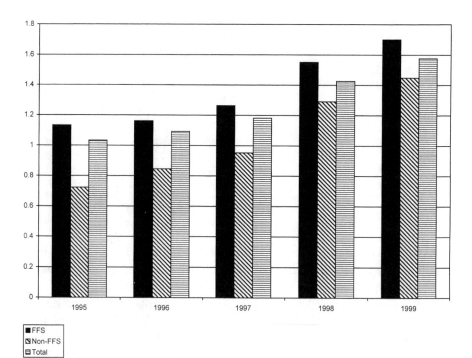

Figure 4.2
Controller/reliever copayment ratios by plan type and year

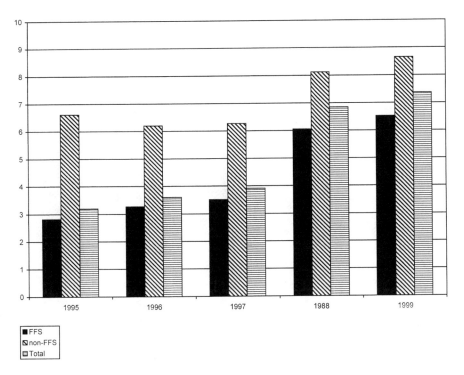

Figure 4.3
Trends in asthma medication copayments by plan type

medication typically sold as a generic), ranged from $2 to $12 across plans.

Figure 4.4 reports the trend in the ratio of total payments (third-party payer plus patient copayment) for controller versus reliever prescription drug claims alongside the trend in the ratio of patient out-of-pocket copayments for controller versus reliever medications. Both ratios show an upward trend, largely reflecting the increased use of controller medications. Figure 4.4 clearly indicates, however, that between 1995 and 1999, the total payment ratio rose at a steeper rate than the copayment ratio. This trend suggests that, although large employers and health plans were using copayments to help manage rising prescription drug costs, at least between 1995 and 1999 they appeared to be absorbing proportionately more of the cost increase than they transferred to beneficiaries in the form of higher copayments. Put another way, the practice of medicine improved in the sense of both FFS and non-FFS beneficiaries increasing the controller/reliever

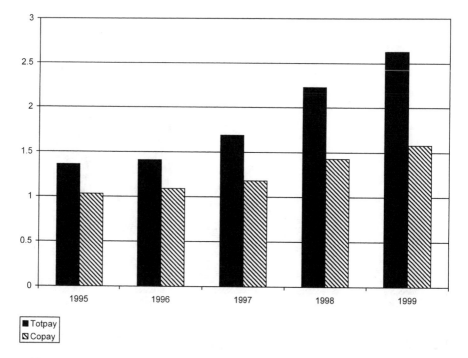

Figure 4.4
Trends in total payment versus copayment ratios

utilization ratio, and while beneficiaries experienced increases in controller/reliever copayment ratios, third-party payers bore an even larger increase in controller/reliever payments.

Average copayments for outpatient visits, emergency room visits, and inpatient visits also differed between non-FFS and FFS plans (table 4.3). Although statistically significant, copayments for outpatient visits and emergency room visits were fairly similar across non-FFS and FFS plans. By contrast, copayments for inpatient stays were significantly and materially higher among patients covered by FFS plans than were those covered by non-FFS plans ($16.12 versus $2.78, respectively, $p <$ .001). Hence, while non-FFS plans had significantly higher copayment rates for prescription drugs relative to FFS plans, the opposite took place in terms of inpatient copayments.

Medication Use
Table 4.4 summarizes the medication use of asthma patients covered by non-FFS and FFS health plans. Patients covered by FFS plans have a

Table 4.4
Annualized asthma medication claims by insurance plan type, 1995–2000

	FFS	Non-FFS	Total	p
N	44,926	18,305	63,231	NA
Ratio of controller to reliever	1.49	1.17	1.40	<.01
Number of asthma prescriptions	4.89	4.17	4.68	<.01
Bronchodilators	0.71	0.37	0.61	<.01
Oral steroids	0.45	0.45	0.45	0.69
SABAs	2.14	2.11	2.13	0.20
Inhaled steroids	1.22	0.90	1.13	<.01
Luekotriene modifiers	0.24	0.28	0.25	<.01
Anticholinergics	0.12	0.05	0.10	<.01
Estimated days of therapy				
Bronchodilators	21.99	10.43	18.64	<.01
Oral steroids	5.91	4.59	5.53	<.01
SABAs	46.44	41.75	45.09	<.01
Inhaled steroids	30.19	20.96	27.51	<.01
Luekotriene modifiers	8.89	9.09	8.94	0.61
Anticholinergics	2.89	1.07	2.36	<.01
Units dispensed				
Bronchodilators	34.05	14.86	28.50	<.01
Oral steroids	18.65	18.16	18.51	0.44
SABAs	78.01	79.50	78.44	0.37
Inhaled steroids	31.33	21.46	28.47	<.01
Luekotriene modifiers	12.73	12.44	12.65	0.63
Anticholinergics	5.26	2.36	4.42	<.01
Selection of asthma medication				
Bronchodilators	15.94%	9.66%	14.12%	<.01
Oral steroids	23.71%	26.42%	24.50%	<.01
SABAs	76.57%	80.63%	77.75%	<.01
Inhaled steroids	35.00%	31.95%	34.11%	<.01
Luekotriene modifiers	5.88%	6.62%	6.09%	<.01
Anticholinergics	4.14%	2.13%	3.56%	<.01

higher ratio of controller-to-reliever medications than patients in non-FFS plans (1.49 versus 1.17, $p < .001$), as well as a higher number of annualized asthma prescriptions (4.89 versus 4.17, $p < .001$). With the exception of leukotriene modifiers (the most recent new therapeutic agents), patients in FFS plans have more days of therapy and higher units dispensed for each therapeutic class of asthma medication than do patients in non-FFS plans ($p < .001$ for all comparisons). For leukotriene modifiers, days of therapy and units dispensed were higher for asthma patients covered by non-FFS plans ($p < .001$).

The most commonly prescribed asthma medications were the short-acting beta-agonists (SABAs). Patients in non-FFS plans were somewhat more likely than patients in FFS plans to be prescribed SABAs, oral steroids, and leukotriene modifiers; they were less likely to be prescribed bronchodilators, inhaled steroids, and anticholinergics ($p < .001$ for all comparisons).

Health Care Utilization

Table 4.5 reports the nonprescription drug health care utilization of patients in non-FFS and FFS plans. For each measure—emergency room visits, hospitalizations, hospital days, and outpatient visits—annualized utilization was higher in FFS plans than it was in non-FFS plans ($p = 0.09$ for emergency room visits). Thus, despite higher controller/reliever medication ratios, health care utilization was higher in FFS plans than it was in non-FFS plans. This association is likely to be confounded, however, by the greater average age and level of disease severity of patients covered by FFS plans (table 4.2).

VII. Econometric Findings

FFS Model

Table 4.6 reports the results of a multinomial logit model of the log odds of a patient receiving controller medication alone, or a controller and a reliever (combination therapy), relative to a reliever alone. Residents of the North Central region are significantly less likely to be treated with controllers alone or a combination of controllers and relievers than with relievers alone ($p < 0.01$). Females were significantly less likely to receive a combination treatment rather than a reliever-only treatment.

Table 4.5
Annualized per–beneficiary, asthma-related health care utilization by insurance plan type, 1995–2000

	FFS	Non-FFS	Total	p
N	44,926	18,305	63,231	NA
Measures of health care use				
Emergency room visits	0.38	0.37	0.38	0.09
Hospitalizations	0.08	0.05	0.07	<.01
Hospital days	0.36	0.23	0.32	<.01
Outpatient visits	5.46	1.40	4.29	<.01

Table 4.6
Multinomial logit model of medication selection: patients in FFS plans[a]

	Controller Alone		Controller + reliever	
	Parameter estimate	Pr > | t |	Parameter estimate	Pr > | t |
Intercept	−3.4707	<0.001	−2.2667	<0.001
Demographics				
Region North central	−0.3932	<0.001	−0.1591	0.0020
Region Northeast	−0.0290	0.8430	−0.0014	0.9900
Region West	−0.1649	0.1410	−0.0199	0.8070
Female	−0.0119	0.7700	−0.1062	<0.001
Adult	0.8893	<0.001	0.2170	<0.001
Clinical characteristics				
Allergic rhinitis	0.5128	<0.001	0.6086	<0.001
Migraine	−0.0270	0.7380	−0.0390	0.5220
Depression	−0.1795	0.0060	−0.0067	0.8850
GI disorders	−0.0537	0.2740	−0.1022	0.0050
Sinusitis	−0.0655	0.1520	0.0110	0.7400
Anxiety disorders	−0.1843	0.1320	−0.2209	0.0150
3-digit ICD-9 codes	0.0483	<0.001	0.0481	<0.001
County characteristics				
County average income $15–20K	0.2960	0.3290	−0.0804	0.6810
County average income $20–25K	0.4274	0.1550	0.0241	0.9010
County average income $25–35K	0.3661	0.2240	0.0713	0.7140
County average income >$35K	0.8503	0.0050	0.1602	0.4170
Copay variables				
Ratio of controller/reliever copayment	−0.0667	0.5030	0.0308	0.6820
Tax provider ID controller, %	6.4705	<0.001	1.1769	0.1840
Tax provider ID combination, %	1.0605	0.0320	4.1513	<0.001
Chi2(3)[b]	60.3200	<0.001	164.5700	<0.001
LR chi2(38)	1816.3600	<0.001		
Psuedo-R2	0.0341			
Number of observations	26,379			

[a]Reference category is reliever alone.
[b]Chi-square test for significance of copay variables.

Adults were more likely to receive a controller alone or a combination treatment (with the former being particularly large) than a reliever-only treatment.

We also included county-level variables from the census as proxies for the income of patients—variables not available directly from the claims. Living in a county with the highest category of average income (> $35,000) significantly increased the odds of receiving a controller-only treatment but had no significant effect on combination treatment relative to reliever-only treatments. None of the other county characteristic income variables was statistically significant.

The presence of allergic rhinitis increased the odds of getting a controller alone or a combination therapy relative to reliever-only therapy. Comorbidities of migraine or sinusitis had no significant impact on choice of drug therapy. Depression reduced the odds of getting controller-only therapy relative to reliever alone but had no significant impact on combination therapy. The presence of an anxiety disorder increased the odds of getting a combination therapy ($p < 0.02$) but had no significant impact on the odds of receiving a controller alone. The number of unique three-digit ICD-9 codes was positively associated with the odds of getting a controller alone or a controller plus reliever relative to reliever-only therapy.

The ratio of plan mean controller to mean reliever copay had no significant impact on drug treatment choice ($p > 0.50$). In results not shown in a table or figure, this lack of significance persisted when mean copays were entered separately in levels or in various other forms. On the other hand, the medication ratios measuring physician/provider prescribing preferences for controller alone ($p < 0.01$) or for combination treatment ($p < 0.01$) were positive, large, and highly significant determinants for the probability of the patient receiving that therapy relative to reliever-only therapy. In terms of cross-effects, only physician/provider prescribing preferences for combination therapy positively and significantly affected the probability of a patient receiving controller-only therapy; physician/provider preferences for controller-only therapy had no significant impact on the patient's probability of receiving combination treatment ($p = 0.184$). The chi-square test statistic for the null hypothesis that coefficient estimates on the copay and physician/provider prescribing preference variables are simultaneously equal to zero indicate decisive rejection in both equations ($p < 0.01$).

Non-FFS Model

Table 4.7 reports the results of the corresponding multinomial logit model for patients in non-FFS plans. Living in the West reduced the odds of receiving either controller-only or combination treatment relative to reliever-only therapy. Residents of the North Central region were more likely to receive combination treatment but not controller-only therapy, relative to reliever alone treatment. As in the FFS case, females were significantly less likely to receive combination therapy, relative to reliever-only therapy, and adults were more likely to receive a controller alone or a combination therapy (with the former being particularly large), relative to reliever-only treatment. None of the county-level income variables from the census was statistically significant.

The presence of allergic rhinitis significantly increased the odds of getting controller-only or combination therapy relative to reliever-only treatment; the effects of other comorbidities were similar in this non-FFS regression to those in the FFS analysis. Higher numbers of unique three-digit ICD-9 codes significantly increased the odds of getting a controller-only or combination therapy relative to reliever-only treatment.

As with the FFS model, the ratio of plan mean controller to mean reliever copayment had no significant impact on the probability of receiving controller-only therapy, although it did have a positive and significant impact on the odds of receiving combination treatment. On the other hand, both medication percentages measuring provider prescribing preferences were highly significant determinants of the probability of a patient receiving the corresponding therapy; while these own effects were positive and significant, both cross-effects were not statistically significant. The chi-square test statistics for the null hypothesis that coefficients on the copay and provider prescriber preference variables simultaneously equal zero indicate decisive rejection in both equations ($p < 0.01$).

Turning now to the log total expenditure regressions for FFS (table 4.8) and non-FFS (table 4.9) beneficiaries, we provide parameter estimates with and without the sample selectivity adjustments for each of the three treatment arms. In the FFS regressions of table 4.8, we note first that parameter estimates on the lambdas (conditional expected values of the residuals derived from each of multinomial logistic equations) are negative and statistically significant (all $p < 0.001$). Not surprisingly, differences between the selectivity-adjusted and unadjusted parameter estimates are particularly large for those variables significantly affecting prescriber therapy in the first-stage multinomial logit equations. For example, coefficient estimates on the adult variable in all three equations are much smaller in the selectivity-adjusted than in the unadjusted regressions; this finding also holds for the allergic rhinitis variable, where sign changes occur.

However, when a Hausman test is conducted to test whether the coefficient estimates differ significantly in the selectivity-adjusted and unadjusted OLS regressions with the FFS sample, the null hypothesis of parameter equality is not rejected. Indeed, the test statistic is negative, a reflection of the fact that the difference in diagonal elements of the variance-covariance matrices can be negative in given samples, even though asymptotically they are positive in expectation.

In terms of the non-FFS sample (table 4.9), results are qualitatively similar to those in the FFS population. In particular, estimates of the three lambdas are negative and significant in all three treatment equations ($p < 0.001$), with the exception of the reliever-only equation, where the negative estimate is not statistically significant. Two of the three Hausman test statistics on parameter equality in the selectivity-adjusted and unadjusted OLS regressions are positive, but in all three cases the null hypothesis is not rejected.

VIII.   Discussion and Limitations

This study describes the patterns of medication use among patients with asthma, factors affecting the type of drug therapy prescribed for these patients, and the effects on total health care expenditures using a data set containing medical claims and encounters for more than 63,000 asthma patients. The average controller-to-reliever ratios were found to be greater than 1 for members of non-FFS (1.17) *and* FFS (1.49) plans. The controller/reliever medication ratio has been consistently rising over time, suggesting that the clinical practices it embodies reflects a considerable degree of acceptance of the consensus guidelines and the supporting research literature.

Holding other factors equal, one would theoretically expect higher relative prices for controller-to-reliever medicines to be associated with a lower controller-to-reliever ratio. However, teasing this conclusion out of the data statistically is complex. Shifts in the composition of drugs in the controller and reliever classes over time and changes in plan design could cause the ratio of controller-to-reliever copays either

Table 4.7
Multinomial logit model of medication selection: patients in non-FFS plans[a]

	Controller alone		Controller + reliever	
	Parameter estimate	Pr > |t|	Parameter estimate	Pr > |t|
Intercept	−6.1203	<0.001	−5.2240	<0.001
Demographics				
Region: North Central	−0.2239	0.0880	−0.1658	0.0440
Region: Northeast	−0.2124	0.0960	−0.0735	0.3350
Region: West	−0.2940	0.0170	−0.3179	<0.001
Female	−0.0941	0.2870	−0.1897	<0.001
Adult	1.1020	<0.001	0.2973	<0.001
Clinical characteristics				
Allergic rhinitis	0.8721	<0.001	0.7965	<0.001
Migraine	−0.0033	0.9870	0.1745	0.2130
Depression	0.0975	0.5540	−0.1856	0.1160
GI disorders	−0.0568	0.6290	−0.1773	0.0230
Sinusitis	0.0685	0.5400	0.0651	0.3690
Anxiety disorders	−0.6812	0.0450	−0.3315	0.1250
3-digit ICD-9 codes	0.0667	<0.001	0.0632	<0.001
County characteristics				
County average income $15–20K	−0.2739	0.5990	−0.2224	0.5050
County average income $20–25K	−0.1448	0.7660	−0.1310	0.6770
County average income $25–35K	−0.1357	0.7770	−0.2558	0.4080
County average income >$35K	−0.3545	0.4770	−0.3857	0.2280
Copay variables				
Ratio of controller/ reliever copayments	0.0816	0.7120	0.6444	<0.001
Tax ID prescriber controller, %	11.4306	0.0030	1.0697	0.6640
Tax ID prescriber combination, %	6.6881	0.0650	11.1009	<0.001
Chi2(3)	16.1400	0.0011	53.6800	<0.001
LR chi2(38)	598.6700	<0.001		
Psuedo-R2	0.0463			
Number of observations	6,768			

[a]Reference category is reliever alone.

Table 4.8
Log-linear regression results: patients in FFS plans [dependent variable: log(total payments)][a]

	Controller alone				Controller + reliever				Reliever alone			
	Selectivity adjusted		Not adjusted		Selectivity adjusted		Not adjusted		Selectivity adjusted		Not adjusted	
	Parameter estimate	Pr > |t|	Parameter estimate	Pr > |t|	Parameter estimate	Pr > |t|	Parameter estimate	Pr > |t|	Parameter estimate	Pr > |t|	Parameter estimate	Pr > |t|
Intercept	1.9666	0.1070	6.0066	<0.001	5.1129	<0.001	6.1208	<0.001	2.1427	<0.001	5.0938	<0.001
Demographics												
Region: North Central	0.2803	<0.001	0.0633	0.1480	0.2251	<0.001	0.0277	0.2860	0.2460	<0.001	-0.0547	0.1360
Region: Northeast	0.1217	0.3370	0.0510	0.6300	0.0421	0.5890	-0.0277	0.6590	-0.0985	0.3030	-0.1831	0.0160
Region: West	0.0961	0.2430	-0.0021	0.9790	0.0357	0.6270	-0.0488	0.2720	-0.0528	0.5290	-0.1999	<0.001
Female	-0.0138	0.6880	-0.0282	0.3620	0.0364	0.1000	0.0018	0.9160	0.0295	0.4590	0.0208	0.2720
Adult	0.0208	0.8410	0.6823	<0.001	0.2500	0.0010	0.6550	<0.001	0.1375	0.0510	0.6722	<0.001
Clinical characteristics												
Allergic rhinitis	-0.1254	0.0030	0.1099	0.0010	-0.1567	<0.001	0.1311	<0.001	-0.0451	0.0180	0.1312	<0.001
Migraine	-0.0165	0.7140	-0.0320	0.5810	0.0102	0.8330	-0.0150	0.6480	-0.0002	0.9950	-0.0284	0.5050
Depression	0.3995	<0.001	0.3139	<0.001	0.3262	<0.001	0.2709	<0.001	0.4994	<0.001	0.4013	<0.001
GI disorders	0.0789	0.0090	0.0648	0.0710	0.1248	<0.001	0.0992	<0.001	0.0661	0.1720	0.0460	0.0640
Sinusitis	0.0539	0.0510	0.0222	0.5120	-0.0033	0.8630	-0.0139	0.4530	0.0220	0.3810	-0.0107	0.6360
Anxiety disorders	0.1709	0.1370	0.0651	0.4730	0.2036	0.0100	0.0827	0.1090	0.3699	<0.001	0.2874	<0.001
3-digit ICD-9 codes	0.0877	<0.001	0.1055	<0.001	0.0763	<0.001	0.0986	<0.001	0.1119	<0.001	0.1324	<0.001
County characteristics												
County average income $15–20 K	-0.1565	0.6690	-0.0311	0.8940	0.0583	0.6350	0.0944	0.3860	0.0111	0.9420	0.1220	0.3730
County average income $20–25 K	-0.2616	0.4660	-0.0493	0.8310	-0.0396	0.7390	0.0696	0.5190	-0.0803	0.5820	0.1146	0.4000
County average income $25–35 K	-0.1384	0.6950	0.0375	0.8710	-0.0055	0.9670	0.0906	0.4010	-0.0379	0.8140	0.1104	0.4190
County average income >$35 K	-0.4295	0.2400	-0.0510	0.8270	-0.2139	0.1420	0.0553	0.6140	-0.3223	0.0290	0.0816	0.5560

Correlations						
Lambda (1)	-3.1896	<0.001	-7.0098	<0.001	-8.9698	<0.001
Lambda (2)	-10.5181	<0.001	-4.1839	<0.001	-8.2394	<0.001
Lambda (3)	-7.8338	<0.001	-5.4709	<0.001	-3.1968	<0.001
R-square	0.4597		0.4791			
Hausman test statistic	-13.9200	<0.001	-189.900	<0.001	62.0700	<0.001
Number of observations	3,903		11,427		11,049	

[a] Lambda is the conditional expected values of the residuals derived from the multinomial logit model of controller alone or controller + reliever, relative to reliever alone. P-values are derived from bootstrapped standard errors.

Table 4.9
Log-linear regression results: patients in non-FFS plans [dependent variable: log(total payments)][a]

| | Controller alone | | | | Controller + reliever | | | | Reliever alone | | | |
| | Selectivity adjusted | | Not adjusted | | Selectivity adjusted | | Not adjusted | | Selectivity adjusted | | Not adjusted | |
	Parameter estimate	Pr > |t|	Parameter estimate	Pr > |t|	Parameter estimate	Pr > |t|	Parameter estimate	Pr > |t|	Parameter estimate	Pr > |t|	Parameter estimate	Pr > |t|
Intercept	3.1781	0.0660	5.6622	<0.001	4.0577	<0.001	3.5437	<0.001	3.7828	<0.001	4.5272	<0.001
Demographics												
Region: North Central	-0.0192	0.9200	-0.0674	0.5690	0.0679	0.4200	0.0688	0.2240	-0.0722	0.1220	-0.0908	0.1640
Region: Northeast	0.0627	0.7480	-0.0121	0.9220	0.1229	0.0640	0.1263	0.1500	-0.0072	0.9330	0.0157	0.8020
Region: West	-0.3234	0.0040	-0.3268	0.0030	-0.1499	0.0650	-0.1729	0.0390	-0.2879	<0.001	-0.2616	<0.001
Female	-0.0143	0.8840	0.0329	0.6670	0.0515	0.3350	0.0520	0.3010	-0.0028	0.9630	-0.0105	0.7990
Adult	0.0170	0.9550	0.4876	<0.001	0.5631	<0.001	0.6438	<0.001	0.8801	<0.001	0.7813	<0.001
Clinical characteristics												
Allergic rhinitis	0.2900	0.1590	0.1509	0.0840	0.2727	0.0210	0.3353	<0.001	0.2532	0.0060	0.0820	0.2230
Migraine	0.1048	0.4700	-0.0253	0.8820	0.0991	0.4890	0.1046	0.1190	0.0926	0.5090	0.0606	0.6120
Depression	0.4014	<0.001	0.5120	<0.001	0.2330	<0.001	0.2548	0.0020	0.6096	<0.001	0.5847	<0.001
GI disorders	0.0911	0.3520	0.1856	0.0680	0.1223	0.0060	0.1212	0.0160	0.1177	0.0610	0.1100	0.0680
Sinusitis	-0.0216	0.8150	-0.0048	0.9590	0.0600	0.1570	0.0607	0.0850	-0.0919	0.0740	-0.1036	0.0750
Anxiety disorders	0.1594	0.7060	0.0599	0.8400	0.1935	0.1880	0.1409	0.2510	0.1276	0.1330	0.2035	0.2150
3-digit ICD-9 codes	0.1413	<0.001	0.1277	<0.001	0.1249	<0.001	0.1292	<0.001	0.1871	<0.001	0.1792	<0.001
County characteristics												
County average income $15–20 K	-0.1889	0.6200	-0.2485	0.5700	0.2593	0.4400	0.2088	0.3820	-0.2283	0.6180	-0.1431	0.6050
County average income $20–25 K	-0.4244	0.2990	-0.4548	0.2640	0.1860	0.5540	0.1668	0.3830	-0.0160	0.9720	0.0184	0.9440
County average income $25–35 K	-0.5821	0.2100	-0.5504	0.1730	0.1211	0.7070	0.0628	0.7520	-0.0408	0.9310	-0.0328	0.8990
County average income >$35 K	-0.4976	0.2950	-0.5362	0.2040	0.2382	0.4620	0.1771	0.4640	0.0865	0.8570	0.0843	0.7510

Correlations						
Lambda (1)	-2.3181	0.0000	-3.4653	0.0010	-1.1454	0.4450
Lambda (2)	-5.6860	0.0000	-2.1676	<0.001	-3.9541	<0.001
Lambda (3)	-7.3977	0.0000	-5.0881	<0.001	-1.9950	<0.001
R-square	0.4563		0.3806		0.3872	
Hausman test statistic	16.2200	0.4381	-4.8800	>0.999	3.3300	0.9997
Number of observations	711		2,881		3,176	

[a] Lambda is the conditional expected values of the residuals derived from the multinomial logit model of controller alone or controller + reliever, relative to reliever alone. P-values are derived from bootstrapped standard errors.

to rise or to fall over time. After controlling for other variables, we do not find a statistically significant relationship between out-of-pocket copayments and asthma treatment patterns. Figure 4.4 indicates that total payments (third-party payer plus patient copay) have been rising more rapidly than copayments only, suggesting that health plans and large employers are reluctant to increase copayments for covered beneficiaries at the same rate that total payments have increased. In this sense and over this 1995–1999 period, health plans and payers have contributed to greater diffusion of guideline-compatible treatments that favor increases in the controller-to-reliever ratio.

The observation that the prescribing of all classes of asthma medications (except leukotriene modifiers) was greater among members of FFS plans is generally consistent with the findings that these patients are sicker than their counterparts in non-FFS plans, as measured by the number of comorbid conditions and higher levels of health care utilization. Asthma patients covered by FFS health plans made more extensive use of all other types of health services that we examined, including inpatient hospitalizations, use of emergency services, and ambulatory visits.

The principal objective of this study has been to examine whether and how the characteristics of health plan coverage as part of the employee benefits program affects the therapy selection decision among patients with asthma. Most of the clinical literature now suggests that patients with asthma experience more favorable clinical courses when they make regular use, often several times daily, of inhaled corticosteriods, leukotriene modifiers, and other medications that control inflammation and reversible airway disease. In the descriptive analysis, we found that the controller-to-reliever ratio continued to rise (and its increase even accelerated in recent years) despite rising medication copays. However, this apparent association between mean copayments at the plan level and plan-level controller-to-reliever ratios is potentially endogenous. For example, if mean copayments are higher for controller medications than they are for reliever medications, growing use of controllers would result in a rising mean copayment ratio for controller-to-reliever medications. That is, at the plan level, the direction of influence between the controller-to-reliever copayments and the controller-to-reliever ratio could go in either direction, or even both ways.

To reduce the endogeneity problem, we examined the effect of plan-level copayment variables on individual treatment choices. When we did so, no statistically significant association was found. It is possible that this lack of association resulted from an understatement of the size of out-of-pocket copayments. This understatement is due to the averaging of patient copays across asthma drugs and years at the plan level, an effort we undertook to reduce the number of degrees of freedom consumed by plan-, drug-, and year-specific copayments. Most of the large copayment increases have occurred since 1999. Plans that instituted large copayment increases for certain asthma drugs may indeed have shifted asthma treatment patterns. In our analysis, however, these more recent changes were aggregated with the earlier experience of patients where copayment changes were not as common nor as large. Thus, we expect that a downward bias exists in our estimate of the copayment effect and that it deserves further scrutiny. We have re-estimated our models using only 1998–2000 data, and while we obtained results on the copay variables that trended more toward becoming statistically significant, they were not significant at usual p values. We suspect that these copay variables will become more significant as additional years of post-2000 data are added to the sample.

On the other hand, we found that physician/provider prescribing patterns were strongly associated with patient treatment patterns, although the nature of this association differed somewhat for patients in FFS and non-FFS plans. We leave it for future research to assess whether (controlling for physician/practice prescribing preferences) differences in copayment benefit design across plans serviced by the same physician/practice result in statistically different treatment patterns. Of course, it is possible instead that physician/practice effects are dominant regardless of the variation in the copayment benefit designs of the plans covering the patients they treat. Resolution of this issue will have important implications for the effectiveness of plan design in controlling health care costs.

In addition to the specific statistical issues already discussed, the conclusions from our analysis should be viewed in light of the limitations common to most retrospective studies. In particular, although we have attempted to correct for selection bias associated with patients having higher versus lower controller-to-reliever ratios, other sources of selection bias may remain. For example, the MarketScan™ claims data used in the analysis lack clinical measures of symptom severity (e.g., results of spirometry tests). In addition, missing data on within-region location (e.g., rural, urban, suburban) could have introduced bias because of geographical variations in asthma treatment practice patterns.

Although future work is unlikely to be able to control for all sources of selection bias in retrospective database studies of the type reported here, the physician/provider prescribing pattern variables appear to offer promise as identifying variables. For example, future work could use instrumental variables or parametric selection models to control for unobserved factors associated with both treatment selection and outcomes when examining the effects of asthma treatments on health care utilization. This general approach is also likely to have broad applicability to other medical conditions and treatments.

Notes

Research support from the Ad Hoc Committee on the Economics of the Pharmaceutical Industry for Medstat and the Massachusetts Institute of Technology Program on the Pharmaceutical Industry is gratefully acknowledged. The opinions and views expressed in this paper are those only of the authors and do not necessarily reflect those of the research sponsors or of the institutions with whom the authors are affiliated. The authors would like to thank Mark Pauly for his thoughtful comments.

1. See Zeckhauser (1970) for a seminal discussion. For more recent analyses, see the exchanges among Nyman (1999), Blomqvist (2001), and Manning and Marquis (1996, 2001).

2. For evidence from the RAND Health Insurance Experiment, see Newhouse and the Insurance Experiment Group (1993); Manning et al. (1986); Leibowitz, Manning, and Newhouse (1985); and Marquis (1985). More recent evidence for a more aged population is given in Feenberg and Skinner (1994).

3. The term *copayment* typically refers to fixed payments by the individual for service received (e.g., $5 for each generic prescription); *coinsurance* typically refers to a fixed percentage payment by the individual (e.g., 20 percent of the retail price of the drug). In this paper, we use the term *copayment* to refer to any out-of-pocket payments by consumers for drugs or other services.

4. See Berndt (2002); see also Berndt (2001).

5. See National Institute for Health Care Management (2002).

6. For policies and the impact of changing prescription drug cost-sharing provisions in Canada, see Alan et al. (2002), Grootendorst (2002), Poirier et al. (1998), and Tamblyn et al. (2001).

7. For further discussion, see Berndt (2002) and the references cited therein.

8. See Pharmacy Benefit Management Institute (2001).

9. For related empirical evidence (much of it quite dated), see Harris et al. (1990); Johnson et al. (1997); Leibowitz, Manning, and Newhouse (1985); Marquis (1985); and Smith (1993).

10. For related empirical analyses, see Keeler et al. (1985), Leibowitz et al. (1985), and Newhouse and the Insurance Experiment Group (1993).

11. See, for example, Levine, Campen, Millares, and Barrueta (2000).

12. See Gottlieb, Belser, and O'Connor (1995); Frischer et al. (1999); and Shelley et al. (2000).

13. See Jain and Golish (1996); Majeed, Ferguson, and Field (1999); Nestor et al. (1998); and Suissa et al. (1994).

14. See Majeed, Ferguson, and Field (1999); Nestor et al. (1998); Suissa et al. (1994); Laumann and Bjornson (1998); and Donahue et al. (1997).

15. See Frischer et al. (1999) and Shelley et al. (2000).

16. See, for example, Gottlieb, Belser, and O'Connor (1995).

17. For further details, see D'Hoore, Bouckaert, and Tilquin (1996).

18. See, for example, D'Hoore, Bouckaert, and Tilquin (1996) and Beddhu et al. (2000).

References

Alan, Sule, Thomas F. Crossley, Paul Grootendorst, and Michael R. Veall (2002). "The Effects of Drug Subsidies on Out-of-Pocket Prescription Drug Expenditures by Seniors: Regional Evidence from Canada," *Journal of Health Economics*, 21(5):805–826.

Beddhu, Srinivasan, Frank J. Bruns, Melissa Saul, Patricia Seddon, and Mark L. Zeidel (2000). "A Simple Comorbidity Scale Predicts Clinical Outcomes and Costs in Dialysis Patients," *American Journal of Medicine*, 108(8):609–613.

Berndt, Ernst R. (2001). "The U.S. Pharmaceutical Industry: Why Major Growth in Times of Cost Containment?" *Health Affairs*, 20(2):100–114.

Berndt, Ernst R. (2002). "Pharmaceuticals in U.S. Health Care: Determinants of Quantity and Price," *Journal of Economic Perspectives*, 16(4):45–66.

Blomqvist, Ake (2001). "Does the Economics of Moral Hazard Need to Be Revisited? A Comment on the Paper by John Nyman," *Journal of Health Economics*, 20(2):283–288.

Bourguignon, Francois, Martin Fournier, and Marc Gurgand (2001). "Selection Bias Correction Based on the Multinomial Logit Model," Center for Research on Econometrics and Statistics (Paris), unpublished working paper, December 27.

D'Hoore W. A. Bouckaert, and C. Tilquin (1996). "Practical Considerations on the Use of the Charlson Comorbidity Index with Administrative Data Bases," *Journal of Clinical Epidemiology* 49(12):1429–1433.

Donahue, J. G., S. T. Weiss, J. M. Livingston, M. A. Goetsch, D. K. Greineder, R. Platt (1997). "Inhaled Steroids and the Risk of Hospitalization for Asthma," *Journal of the American Medical Association*, 277(11):877–891.

Feenberg, Daniel, and Jonathan Skinner (1994). "The Risk and Duration of Catastrophic Health Care Expenditures," *Review of Economics and Statistics*, 76:333–347.

Frischer, M., H. Heathe, S. Chapman, J. Norwood, J. Bashford, and D. Millson (1999). "Should the Corticosteroid to Bronchodilator Ratio be Promoted as a Quality Prescribing Marker?" *Public Health*, 113(5):247–250.

Gottlieb D. J., A. S. Belser, G. T. O'Connor (1995). "Poverty, Race, and Medication Use Are Correlates of Asthma Hospitalization Rates," *Chest*, 108:28–35.

Grootendorst, Paul (2002). "Beneficiary Cost Sharing Under Canadian Provincial Prescription Drug Benefit Programs: History and Assessment," *Canadian Journal of Clinical Pharmacology*, 9(2):79–99.

Harris, B. L., A. Stergachis, and L. D. Ried (1990). "The Effect of Drug Co-payments on Utilization and Cost of Pharmaceuticals in a Health Maintenance Organization," *Medical Care*, 28:907–917.

Jain, P., and J. A. Golish (1996). "Clinical Management of Asthma in the 1990s: Current Therapy and New Directions," *Drugs*, 52(Suppl6):1–11.

Johnson, R. E., M. J. Goodman, M. C. Hornbrook, and M. B. Eldredge (1997). "The Effect of Increased Prescription Drug Cost Sharing on Medical Care Utilization and Expenses of Elderly Health Maintenance Organization Members," *Medical Care*, 35:1119–1131.

Keeler, E. B., R. H. Brook, G. A. Goldberg, C. J. Kamberg, and J. P. Newhouse (1985). "How Free Care Reduced Hypertension in the Health Insurance Experiment," *Journal of the American Medical Association*, 254:1926–1931.

Laumann, J. M., and D. C. Bjornson (1998). "Treatment of Medicaid Patients with Asthma: Comparison with Treatment Guidelines Using Disease-Based Drug Utilization Review Methodology," *Annals of Pharmacotherapy*, 32(12):1290–1294.

Lee, L. F. (1983). "Generalized Econometric Models with Selectivity," *Econometrica*, 51:507–512.

Leibowitz, Arleen, Willard G. Manning, and Joseph P. Newhouse (1985). "The Demand for Prescription Drugs as a Function of Cost Sharing," *Social Science and Medicine*, 21(10):1063–1070.

Levine, Sharon, David Campen, Mirta Millares, and Anthony Barrueta (2000). "Kaiser Permanente's Prescription Drug Benefit," *Health Affairs*, 19(2):17–22.

Majeed, A., J. Ferguson, and J. Field (1999). "Prescribing of Beta-2 Agonists and Inhaled Steroids in England: Trends Between 1992 and 1998, and Association with Material Deprivation, Chronic Illness and Asthma Mortality Rates," *Journal of Public Health Medicine*, 21(4):395–400.

Manning, Willard G., and M. Susan Marquis (1996). "Health Insurance: The Tradeoff Between Risk Pooling and Moral Hazard," *Journal of Health Economics*, 15:609–640.

Manning, Willard G., and M. Susan Marquis (2001). "Health Insurance: Tradeoffs Revisited," *Journal of Health Economics*, 20(2):289–29.

Manning, W. G., K. B. Wells, N. Duan, J. P. Newhouse, and J. E. Ware (1986). "How Cost Sharing Affects the Use of Ambulatory Mental Health Services," *Journal of the American Medical Association*, 256:1930–1934.

Marquis, M. Susan (1985). "Cost-Sharing and Provider Choice," *Journal of Health Economics*, 4:137–157.

National Institute for Health Care Management (2002), *Prescription Drug Expenditures in 2001: Another Year of Escalating Costs*. A report by the National Institute for Health Care Management Research and Educational Foundation, Washington, D.C.

Nestor, A., A. C. Calhoun, M. Dickson, and C. A. Kalik (1998). "Cross-Sectional Analysis of the Relationship Between National Guideline Recommended Asthma Drug Therapy and Emergency/Hospital Use Within a Managed Care Population," *Annals of Allergy Asthma Immunology*, 81(4):327–330.

Newhouse, Joseph P., and the Insurance Experiment Group (1993). *Free for All? Lessons from the RAND Health Insurance Experiment*, Cambridge, Mass.: Harvard University Press.

Nyman, John (1999). "The Economics of Moral Hazard Revisited," *Journal of Health Economics*, 18:811–824.

Pharmacy Benefit Management Institute (2001). *Takeeda-Lilly Prescription Drug Benefit Cost and Plan Design Survey Report*, Tempe, Ariz.: Pharmacy Benefit Management Institute.

Poirier, S., J. LeLorier, V. Page, and A. Lacour (1998). "The Effect of a $2 Co-Payment on Prescription Refill Rates of Quebec Elderly and Its Relationship to Socioeconomic Status," *Canadian Pharmaceutical Journal*, 131:30–34.

Shelley, M., P. Croft, S. Chapman, and C. Pantin (2000). "Is the Quality of Asthma Prescribing, as Measured by the General Practice Ratio of Corticosteroid to Bronchodilator, Associated with Asthma Morbidity?" *Journal of Clinical Epidemiology*, 53(12):1217–1221.

Sin, D. J. V. Tu (2001). "Underuse of Inhaled Steroid Therapy in Elderly Patients with Asthma," *Chest*, 119:720–725.

Smith, D. G. (1993). "The Effects of Co-Payments and Generic Substitution on the Use and Costs of Prescription Drugs," *Inquiry*, 30:189–198.

Stafford, Randall S., Jun Ma, Stan N. Finkelstein, Kenan Haver, and Iain M. Cockburn (2002). "National Trends in Asthma Visits and Asthma Pharmacotherapy, 1978–2002," Palo Alto Calif.: Stanford Center for Research in Disease Prevention, unpublished manuscript, September.

Suissa S., P. Ernst, J. F. Bolvin, R. I. Horwitz, B. Habbick, D. Cockroft, L. Blais, M. McNutt, A. S. Buist, W. O. Spitzer (1994). "A Cohort Analysis of Excess Mortality in Asthma and the Use of Inhaled Beta-Agonists," *American Journal of Respiratory Critical Care Medicine*, 149(3pt1): 604–610.

Tamblyn, R., R. Laprise, J. A. Hanley, M. Abrahamowitz, S. Scott, N. May, J. Hurley, R. Grad, E. Latimer, R. Perreault, P. McLeod, A. Huang, P. Larochelle, and L. Mallet (2001). "Adverse Events Associated with Prescription Drug Cost-Sharing Among Poor and Elderly Persons," *Journal of the American Medical Association*, 285:421–429.

Zeckhauser, Richard J. (1970). "Medical Insurance: A Case Study of the Tradeoff Between Risk Spreading and Appropriate Incentives," *Journal of Economic Theory*, 2:10–26.

5

An Economic Analysis of Health Plan Conversions: Are They in the Public Interest?

Nancy Dean Beaulieu, *Harvard Business School and NBER*

Executive Summary

Over the last decade, managed-care companies have been consolidating on both a regional and national scale. More recently, nonprofit health plans have been converting to for-profit status, and this conversion has frequently occurred as a step to facilitate merger or acquisition with a for-profit company. Some industry observers attribute these managed-care marketplace trends to an industry shakeout resulting from increased competition in the sector. At the same time, these perceived competitive pressures have led to questions about the long-run viability of nonprofit health plans. Furthermore, some industry and government leaders believe that some nonprofits are already conducting themselves like for-profit health plans and question the state premium tax exemption ordinarily accorded to such plans. This paper examines related health policy issues through the lens of a case study of the proposed conversion of the CareFirst Blue Cross Blue Shield company to a for-profit public-stock company and its merger with the Wellpoint Corporation. Company executives and board members argued that CareFirst lacked access to sufficient capital and faced serious threats to its viability as a financially healthy nonprofit health care company. They also argued that CareFirst and its beneficiaries would benefit from merger through enhanced economies of scale and product-line extensions. Critics of the proposed conversion and merger raised concerns about the adverse impacts on access to care, coverage availability, quality of care, safety-net providers, and the cost of health insurance. Analyses demonstrate that CareFirst wields substantial market power in its local market, that it is unlikely to realize cost savings through expanded economies of scale, and that access to capital concerns are largely driven by the perceived need for further expansion through merger and acquisition. Although it is impossible to predict future changes in quality of care for CareFirst, analyses suggest that quality appears to be somewhat lower in for-profit national managed-care companies. Additional research is needed to assess the viability of true nonprofits, the potential effects of nonprofits and for-profit national managed-care plans on the evolution of local insurance and provider markets, and methods for effective oversight of nonprofit health plans.

I.   Introduction

In 1994, the Blue Cross and Blue Shield (BCBS) Association changed its bylaws to allow members to convert to public-stock companies. This touched off a streak of conversions and health plan combinations. To date, fourteen BCBS plans have converted to for-profit plans and a few more have conversions pending. Consolidation has also occurred among BCBS plans; in 1996, there were sixty-three BCBS plans in operation; in 2003, there were forty-one. In many instances, BCBS plans have converted with the explicit intention of being acquired or of merging with another firm; hence conversions and consolidation are intertwined. This situation has certainly been the case for two BCBS plans that have led the consolidation trend. Anthem, Inc. is a publicly traded BCBS plan that was built up through the acquisition of exclusive BCBS licenses in nine states. WellPoint, Inc. began with the conversion of the California Blue Cross Association and has grown to the largest BCBS company, with operations in California, Georgia, and Missouri.[1] Regional consolidation has also occurred among nonprofit BCBS plans (for example, the Regence Group with operations in Washington, Oregon, Utah, and Idaho).

These changes among BCBS Association members have occurred against a backdrop of the growing presence of national managed-care companies and for-profit health plans in the health maintenance organization (HMO) industry. As shown in figures 5.1 and 5.2, HMO enrollment increased 173 percent from 1987 to 2001. Nearly three-quarters of the increase is attributable to enrollment growth in for-profit health plans; 50 percent of the enrollment growth occurred in for-profit national managed-care plans. Some industry analysts have argued that the rise of national managed-care companies has precipitated conversion and consolidation among BCBS plans.

Each of the conversion cases is unique. Local health plan markets are unique, and so the health plans that operate in them evolve with a unique history. Thus, the evaluations of specific conversion petitions (and possible acquisitions and mergers) must take into account factors unique to each market. Some policy issues are common to all conversions, however, and in this paper I develop a framework for analyzing these issues and clarifying the trade-offs faced by policy makers.

Following a general discussion of the policy issues and the development of an analytic framework, I present a case study analysis of a particular conversion petition. In January 2002, the CareFirst Corporation

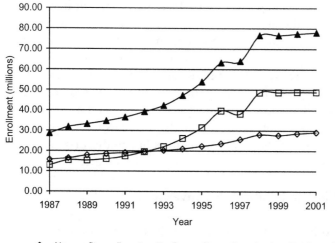

Figure 5.1
HMO enrollment by tax status

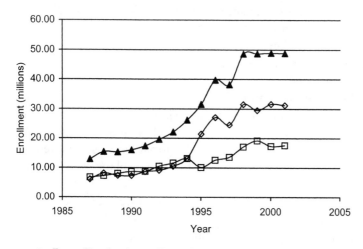

Figure 5.2
HMO enrollment in national versus local or regional for-profit health plans

filed applications to convert to public-stock ownership with insurance
commissioners in the states of Delaware and Maryland, and in the
District of Columbia. CareFirst's conversion application was explicitly
linked to subsequent acquisition by Wellpoint Inc. I present analyses
that were conducted for the public advocacy organization, D.C.
Appleseeds, to support its participation in the formal proceedings in
Washington, D.C. At the end of this paper, I discuss the information
gaps that plague research and policy analysis on this topic, opportunities for health economists to contribute to policy in this arena, and the
limitations and generalizability of my case study research.

II. Policy Issues in Health Plan Conversions

Blue Cross and Blue Shield plans are not the only health plans to convert to public-stock ownership. The BCBS conversion petitions have
sparked the most public debate however, partly because of the special
circumstances in which they were created and because their conversion
typically requires a formal determination by a regulatory official; some
conversions even require legislation. This paper deals specifically with
BCBS conversions; however, several of the health policy issues are germane to other health plan conversions and more generally to the role
of nonprofit organizations in health care.

Origins of the Blue Cross and Blue Shield Plans

Many of the health policy issues that arise in connection with the conversion to for-profit status of BCBS plans relate in some way to the
original creation of the Blue Cross companies. As detailed in
Blackstone and Fuhr (1998), most of the Blue Cross plans were initiated
by the hospital industry in the 1920s and 1930s to provide hospital
insurance at a time when hospitals experienced declining occupancy
rates and escalating operating costs. Typically, these plans were established through state legislation as public-benefit organizations, and
they were intended to serve as insurers of last resort. In enacting legislation to establish the Pennsylvania BC plan in 1937, Representative
Herbert Cohen remarked:

The Legislature of Pennsylvania in approving this law was attempting to meet
a severe need of providing citizens of Pennsylvania with hospital care at a cost
within their means and also of providing hospitals with a source of financial
support which would place them in a more stable financial position and therefore less dependent upon state and local tax funds. The Legislature therefore

was attempting to fill a gap created by commercial insurance companies' underwriting policies which left the mass of Pennsylvania citizens unprotected from hospitalization expenses and hospital bills in many instances unpaid.[2]

The plans were exempted from state income taxes on premiums and in return were subject to various regulations and charged with a public service commitment. Blue Shield plans were created to provide insurance for physician services. The two insurance associations merged into the BCBS Association in 1982.[3]

Nonprofit BCBS Plans and the Public Interest

Because these plans were chartered as tax-exempt organizations for public benefit, state insurance commissioners are obligated to assess whether conversion to a public-stock company is in the public's interest. In addition, in the case in which conversion precedes the sale of a BCBS plan, the insurance commissioner must ascertain that the public receives fair value for the plan from the acquirer.[4, 5] In some instances, the proceeds of the sale are placed in a foundation; these funds are often used to meet the original objectives of the BCBS plans—to provide access to health care services for those in need.[6]

In reaching a judgment on whether conversion advances the public interest, state insurance commissioners are likely to take into account the potential effects of conversion on multiple stakeholders. For example, the insurance commissioner will want to know how conversion will affect insurance coverage for vulnerable populations and reimbursement to providers. This analysis of the effects of conversion will require an understanding of how, if at all, the *behavior* or *conduct* of the health plan might change as a result of the conversion and potential sale or merger. The insurance commissioner may consider at least six dimensions of health plan conduct. Each is discussed in the following subsections. Changes in the conduct of the health plan in any of these areas could influence access to health care, insurance coverage, the quality of the health care services provided, health status in the population, the financial health of providers, and the costs of health insurance to individuals and employers.

Products Offered and Markets Served.   Most health plans offer several different health insurance products, and some of these products are tailored for particular subpopulations. Products may differ on several dimensions: the provider network, reimbursement for care provided by providers not in the network, co-insurance and copayment rates, services covered (i.e., benefit design), and maximum payments under the policy. In some states, nonprofit health plans are required to offer plans in which any person may enroll without regard for the individual's age, employment status, health status, or any other factor that might otherwise cause the individual to be denied health insurance. These plans are sometimes referred to as open enrollment plans. In deciding on the set of health insurance products to offer, health plans make implicit choices about whether to serve certain subpopulations. For example, not all health plans choose to offer a Medicaid or Medicare product; other noteworthy subpopulations include the small-business segment, the individual policy segment, and the Federal Employees Health Benefits Program (FEHBP).

Quality of Care.   Health plans can influence the quality of health care services delivered to enrollees in several ways. Many of these levers require financial outlays by the health plan for patient and physician education, information systems, and program design and administration. For example, health plans may design and implement chronic disease management programs.

Quality of Service.   Health plans have frequent interactions with enrollees about coverage issues, the status of particular claims, and the plan's provider network. The manner in which these inquiries are resolved may not directly affect quality of care but may indirectly affect access to care.

Pricing and Underwriting Practices.   In some states, health insurance premiums for particular managed-care products are community rated, which means that the insurance regulator has eliminated the health plan's pricing decision and requires all plans serving a specific population to charge the same premium. In other states, premiums (and benefit design) for some products are subject to review by the insurance regulator. In yet other states, there is no regulatory oversight of health plan pricing policies. Depending on the regulatory regime of the state in which the health plan is operating, the health plan may be able to adjust premiums based on the risk factors of the group (or individual) to be insured. These are the firms' underwriting policies.

Provider Networks and Reimbursement.   In most states and for most products, health plans have a free hand in deciding which providers to include in their networks and in negotiating the level and the form of reimbursement for services delivered to enrollees.[7] It is frequently noted anecdotally that some health plans reimburse at levels substantially above or below other health plans in the same market. Health plans may institute other policies that make it more or less difficult for the physician to be reimbursed for health care services. For example, some providers criticize utilization review and precertification as burdensome interventions that increase physicians' costs of delivering care and decrease patients' access to care.

Public and Community Health Efforts.   Most health plans earmark some resources for outreach efforts intended to improve the health of community members regardless of enrollment in the health plan. These efforts include measures such as free screening for certain diseases and public health education.

Necessary Conditions for Changes in Health Plan Conduct
Whether the conversion or conversion/sale of a health plan is likely to alter the health plan's conduct on any of the above dimensions hinges on two conditions. First, depending on the regulatory environment and the nature of the market in which the health plan operates, the plan may or may not be able to change its conduct on some of these dimensions. For example, maybe all health plans operating in a particular state, regardless of their tax status, must reimburse hospitals according to the same mandated fee schedule. An alternative potential constraint on health plan conduct may be present in the level of market competition. Consultants to one health plan applying for conversion have argued that the market in which the health plan was operating was so competitive that it effectively limited the prices the health plan could charge and still attract enrollees.[8]

The second condition necessary for a conversion or a conversion/ sale to result in a change of conduct is that such change must be expected to increase the short- or long-term profitability of the health plan. Conceptually, a converting health plan could increase profitability in three ways. First, it could terminate the practice of cross-subsidizing premiums on unprofitable insurance products or subsidizing care delivery by certain providers. Eliminating a subsidy or cross-subsidy could increase profits but only at the expense of one of the stakeholders (i.e., some population of consumers or providers); thus, this type of change in conduct would amount to a value transfer from consumers and/or providers to shareholders.

The second mechanism through which a converting health plan may increase profits is through investment in new products and technologies. Two examples in this category come to mind. Some market observers and participants allege that nonprofit health plans have limited access to capital and therefore may be unable to make the necessary investments that would lead to new products or lower costs. Nonprofit health plans may also be subject to some organizational inertia and that, while they possess the necessary resources and capabilities, they do not feel compelled to innovate. This organizational inertia could be attributable to insulation from competitive pressure afforded by the state tax exemption on premiums. A change in conduct of this nature could lead to value creation because consumers would benefit from new products and reduced costs.

The third mechanism through which a converting health plan may increase profits is through improved efficiency resulting from enhanced accountability and governance structures. In nonprofit organizations, the residual claimants to the surplus created by an organization are unclear. Those who make decisions for the organization do not have a clear objective function; consequently it is difficult to identify suitable performance measures, to structure appropriate incentives, and to hold decision makers accountable. Reducing inefficiency through improved accountability and governance structures is a value-creating activity because it results in services being delivered at the lowest cost to society overall.

Recall that the insurance commissioner must determine whether a conversion is likely to advance the public interest. If the expected changes in health plan behavior do not have the potential to create additional value and are simply a transfer from consumers and providers to prospective shareholders, it would seem difficult to argue that the conversion is in the public interest. On the other hand, if the expected changes in health plan behavior are likely to result in new and better products, conversion may indeed advance public welfare. In all likelihood, a health plan conversion will have the potential for both value creation and value transfer. In these cases, the insurance commissioner must, in essence, make a judgment that involves trade-offs among different stakeholders.

Other Considerations Beyond Changes in Health Plan Conduct

The simple alternatives of approving or denying the conversion petition are more complicated than they might seem at first glance. The
consequences of approving the conversion are not simply the anticipated costs and benefits of changes in health plan conduct; one must
also consider the opportunities afforded by an endowed foundation
charged with the mission of serving the public interest. The consequences of denying the conversion are not simply the preservation of
the status quo. One must consider the factors that prompted the conversion petition in the first place and what they signal about the evolution of the local health care market and the viability of the health plan
petitioning to convert.

To assess whether a foundation could more efficiently execute the
public-service mission of a nonprofit health plan, it is instructive first
to evaluate the extent to which the petitioning health plan is currently
executing this mission and to approximate the resources it requires
(both financial and organizational) to do so. Only then can one determine whether a foundation can accomplish the same task at a lower
cost or implement an expanded mission with the funds available from
the conversion.

Oversight of a nonprofit health plan's execution of its mission is not
typically considered to be in the purview of state insurance regulators
and is largely delegated to board members. Some question surrounds
whether these nonprofit health plans are completely fulfilling their
missions as public-benefit organizations. In written testimony submitted to the Maryland Insurance Administration in March 2002, William
Jews, the chief executive officer (CEO) of the CareFirst Blue Cross Blue
Shield Company explains when and why the Blue Cross Blue Shield of
Maryland (BCBSMD) plan stopped filling the role of insurer of last
resort:

As with other Blues Plans being formed at about the same time, the [Blue
Cross Blue Shield of Maryland plan] was conceived with the goal of
providing affordable health care insurance using "community rating"
principles. This worked effectively at a time when few, if any, commercial
carriers were offering health coverage. In the 1960s, commercial insurance
carriers began entering the health insurance market in earnest and
introduced the concept of "experience rating." As commercial carriers
focused on providing coverage at lower premiums to the healthiest
individuals and groups, Blues Plans like BCBSMD continued to extend
coverage to all comers, including high risk through its community rating

mechanism. As a result, many Blue Plans became known as "insurers of last resort" in their service areas. . . .

That role of insurer of last resort changed in the 1960s when the federal government—in essence—assumed the mantle of insurer of last resort by establishing the Medicare and Medicaid programs to guarantee health covered to the aged and disabled and to provide coverage to the poor. From that point forward, Blues Plans began to compete with commercial insurance carriers and the long-standing expectation that "Blues" would act as the insurer of last resort was greatly minimized. In addition, the continued use by our competitors of experience rating, which gave them an unfair advantage, forced most Blue Plans to abandon community rating in order to survive.

Jews contends that the creation of public insurance programs by the federal government relieved the Blues plans of fulfilling their role as insurers of last resort. If the public-service mission of BCBS plans is limited to the narrow interpretation of providing affordable health insurance using community rating, and if this mission has been abandoned by BCBS plans seeking to convert, then the insurance commissioner's decision about whether to approve a conversion petition is somewhat simplified. Under the current organization and governance structure, the nonprofit plan is receiving a tax exemption while operating in a manner closely resembling that of a for-profit health plan; the foregone tax receipts and the alternative uses of the plan's assets are the opportunity costs of disallowing the conversion and requiring the health plan to continue under the status quo.

The insurance commissioner may decide, however, that the public interest would be better served by going beyond denial of the petition and instituting reform of the health plan governance structures and accountability systems to ensure that it pursues its original mission. Whether or not this approach is the best course of action hinges on two additional analyses: (1) an assessment of whether the mission will be executed more efficiently by a suitably reformed nonprofit health plan or a newly created foundation, and (2) whether either institution is viable in the long run.

In his statements above, Jews asserts that the BCBSMD plan was compelled to abandon its original mission so it could survive competition from commercial insurance carriers. These views are echoed in a recent account of the conversion of the Blue Cross and Blue Shield plan of New York.[9] James Robinson recounts how state regulators destroyed the delicate balancing act of cross-subsidization achieved by Empire BCBS when the regulators allowed commercial insurers to enter the market and attract healthy low-cost enrollees with lower premiums. These actions precipitated an adverse selection spiral that left Empire with the sickest enrollees and the highest costs. In general, the long-term financial viability of an efficient nonprofit is unknown. Research on the regulatory structures that might support a nonprofit health plan and the social efficiency of such regimes is also limited.

The foregoing analysis suggests a framework for guiding research and decision making on health plan conversions (see figure 5.3). Prior to evaluating the potential changes in health plan conduct and the effects of these changes on public welfare, the insurance commissioner might first want to consider whether:

1. The public interest mission of the nonprofit can be achieved more efficiently through a foundation or a health insurance plan.
2. Any organization can faithfully execute this mission and remain financially viable.

After making these assessments, the insurance commissioner must then weigh the costs and benefits to different constituencies of likely changes in health plan conduct.

III. Case Study

In the previous section of this paper, I described, in a generic sense, some of the health policy issues that arise when a nonprofit health plan petitions a state insurance regulator to convert to a public-stock company (potentially to be acquired by another company). In this section, I present some case study research conducted when the CareFirst Blue Cross and Blue Shield Company (with licenses in Delaware, Maryland, and Washington, D.C.) petitioned to convert to a public-stock company, and to be acquired by Wellpoint Health Networks, Inc. I provide a brief description of the CareFirst organization and the events leading up to the conversion petition. Then I summarize the main arguments both for and against the conversion as they have been presented in oral and written testimony, in publicly available reports, and in the public press. Next, I present the results of the analyses of market structure, economies of scale, and

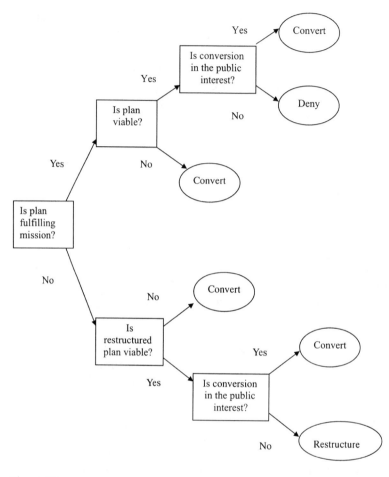

Figure 5.3
Decision calculus for conversions

quality of care. Finally, I report on the outcome of the petition and the research challenges remaining.

Background on CareFirst

CareFirst, Inc. is a holding company with BCBS licenses for Delaware, the District of Columbia, and Maryland. The company was formed in 1998 with the merger of BCBS of Maryland and BCBS of the National Capital Area (District of Columbia). In 2000, BCBS of Delaware became part of CareFirst.

CareFirst is overseen by a central board of directors; William Jews is the CEO of CareFirst and CEO of each of the three subsidiaries that make up CareFirst: Group Hospitalization and Medical Services Inc.— GHMSI (the D.C. Blues), CareFirst of Maryland (the Maryland Blues), and BCBSD (the Delaware Blues). The CareFirst corporation offers a wide variety of insurance products in these three jurisdictions.

In November 2001, CareFirst entered into a merger agreement with Wellpoint Health Networks, Inc. of California. To consummate this merger agreement, CareFirst needed to convert to a for-profit public-stock company. The insurance commissioners in all three jurisdictions in which CareFirst operates needed to approve the conversion petition; however, Maryland was the first jurisdiction to initiate formal proceedings to evaluate the merits of conversion. As part of the proceedings in Maryland and in the District of Columbia, public hearings and discovery were conducted to generate information to inform the public-interest determination. Valuation studies of CareFirst were also initiated.

Summary of Arguments for and Against Conversion

The CareFirst management team and its consultants advanced three primary reasons in support of the conversion petition. First, they cited an inability to access sufficient capital to fund investments that would enhance efficiency, improve customer service, and facilitate the development of new and better products. In the consultant's report and in CareFirst's strategic plan, however, it appeared that the need for capital was largely driven by plans for acquiring other health plans. The need to achieve economies of scale was cited as the primary reason for this acquisition strategy. Second, without these improvements (and larger scale), they contended that CareFirst's long-run viability was uncertain. Approving the conversion would therefore "help to secure the long-term future of the 'Blue' brand in local markets."[10] Third, approving the conversion and merger with Wellpoint would benefit the public because it would result in additional tax receipts (estimated to be $20 million annually) and the creation of a foundation with an endowment of $1.3 billion that would be apportioned to the three jurisdictions.

Those opposing the conversion cited various concerns, many of which related to the future conduct of a for-profit BCBS plan. Concerns about access to care stemmed from the expectation that after conversion, CareFirst would discontinue offering insurance products that served vulnerable populations and that were relatively unprofitable. Some people feared that CareFirst would raise premiums, tighten underwriting practices (abandon guaranteed issue), and narrow the coverage of the insurance policies it continued to offer. Another policy concern related to the potential for skimping on quality. Some providers were not supportive of the conversion petition because they feared reductions in payment rates, increased administrative burden, and a more adversarial relationship. Both providers and consumers feared the loss of a local institution led by members of the community with the long-run interests of the community in mind. Two objections to the conversion were unrelated to anticipated changes in health plan conduct. Some people felt that Wellpoint's offer of $1.3 billion to acquire CareFirst was less than the fair value of CareFirst as an ongoing concern.[11] Finally, many consumers were outraged about the bonuses CareFirst executives were scheduled to receive if the deal went through.

Economic Analyses
Market Structure. CareFirst executives and consultants have suggested in their filings that the markets in which the CareFirst plans operate are so competitive that they constrain their ability to raise premiums or lower quality without losing enrollees to other local health plans. They imply that CareFirst, if it were allowed to convert to for-profit status, would not take such actions (raising premiums or lowering quality) because the loss of enrollment would decrease profits. Traditionally, economists have used market-share summary measures as proxies for market competitiveness. The belief is that greater concentration of market share among a smaller number of firms is likely to result in higher prices.

Computing market shares in practice requires definition of the market and detailed data for each firm. Market definitions can have large effects on both measures of concentration and market shares for individual firms. In this section, I examine the extent of market concentration in the District of Columbia (D.C.) using data on HMO and managed-care enrollment.[12] I am able to obtain relatively complete enrollment data for health plans licensed to do business in D.C.; these detailed data facilitate analyses of market share by consumer segment and product type. However, CareFirst also sells policies in Maryland, Virginia, and Delaware. A complete analysis of the market power possessed by CareFirst would require comparable analyses in these other geographic markets.

D.C. Health Plan Enrollment. Table 5.1 reports the health plan enrollment and market share for each health plan licensed to sell health insurance policies in D.C. for the years 2000 and 2001.[13] In 2001, there were a total of fourteen health plans, most of which fall into one of three categories. Four national for-profit companies (Aetna U.S. Healthcare, AMERIGROUP, Cigna, and United Healthcare) did a small amount of business in D.C. (combined market share of roughly 10.1 percent). Three other health plans (George Washington University Health Plan, Optimum Choice, and MD-Individual Practice Association) could be characterized as relatively small regional plans because they operated in a small number of adjacent states. In 2001, these regional plans accounted for 15.6 percent of the market. Four health plans (Health Right Inc., DC Chartered Health Plan, Advantage Health Plan, and Capital Community Health Plan) offered products only in D.C.; together these plans accounted for 3.5 percent of the market.

Table 5.1
Health plan enrollment in the District of Columbia, 2000–2001

	2001		2000	
	Enrollment	Share	Enrollment	Share
Advantage Healthplan	3,194	0.00	3,471	0.00
Aetna U.S. Healthcare (a Maryland corporation)	177,820	0.09	179,469	0.10
AMERIGROUP Maryland, Inc.	12,876	0.01	12,640	0.01
Capital Community Health Plan	28,851	0.02	25,955	0.01
CareFirst BlueChoice Inc.	46,534	0.02	46,525	0.03
Cigna Healthcare Mid-Atlantic, Inc.	1,655	0.00	2,146	0.00
DC Chartered Health Plan, Inc.	26,877	0.01	27,687	0.01
GHMSI	924,798	0.48	879,338	0.47
GW University Health Plan	82,854	0.04	100,980	0.05
Health Right, Inc.	9,168	0.00	4,838	0.00
Kaiser of the Mid-Atlantic	376,877	0.20	389,349	0.21
MD-IPA, Inc.	171,207	0.09	130,064	0.07
Optimum Choice	44,233	0.02	25,612	0.01
Prudential Health Care Plan, Inc.	0	0.00	23,918	0.01
United Healthcare of the Mid-Atlantic, Inc.	1,279	0.00	1,648	0.00
Total	1,908,223		1,853,640	
Herfindahl		0.29		0.29

Omitted from this categorization are two CareFirst plans and the
Kaiser plan. CareFirst operates two health plans in D.C.: CareFirst
BlueChoice (hereafter BlueChoice) and Group Hospitalization and
Medical Services, Inc. (GHMSI). Together these plans represent 50.9
percent of the market; however, GHMSI, with a 48.5 percent share,
dominates in this market. Kaiser Foundation Health Plan has the second largest share of the D.C. market (19.8 percent) and does not fit
neatly into any of the above three categories. It is affiliated with the
only national nonprofit health plan in the United States.

Total health plan enrollment in D.C. grew 2.9 percent from 2000 to
2001. All national for-profit plans (with the exception of AMERI-
GROUP, which gained 200 enrollees) lost market share over this time
period. Prudential Health Care operated a plan in 2000, but it termi-
nated this local plan in 2001 following its acquisition by Aetna Health
Plans. Two regional plans experienced substantial increases in enrollment (MD-IPA grew by 41,000; Optimum Choice grew by 18,600); the
third regional health plan, George Washington University Health Plan,
lost roughly 18,000 enrollees. GHMSI experienced the largest absolute
enrollment gains during this period, adding more than 45,000 enrollees.

D.C. Enrollment by Consumer Segment. As shown in table 5.2,
health plans operating in D.C. sell policies to several different consumer segments; however, enrollment in two of these segments (the
commercial group and Federal Employee Health Benefits Program
[FEHBP] segments) constitutes 91.5 percent of all health insurance
policies sold in D.C. The largest market segment is the commercial
group market, which accounts for 47 percent of all health insurance
policies; GHMSI and BlueChoice together hold a 51 percent share of
this segment. Commercial group products are typically sold to employers (large and small), who in turn offer these health plans as a benefit
to their employees at some fraction of the per-enrollee cost to the
employer.

The second largest segment is FEHBP; the FEHBP segment is very
similar to the commercial group segment because the federal government essentially acts as a large employer. One difference between these
two segments is that any health plan meeting a minimum set of criteria may participate in FEHBP (i.e., offer a health plan to federal
employees); private-sector employers typically contract selectively
with a very small number of health plans. The FEHBP market segment
is nearly as large as the commercial group segment (44 percent of

Table 5.2
Health plan enrollment in D.C. by consumer segment, 2001

	Group	Individual	Medicare	Medicaid	Supplemental Medicare	Other	FEHBP	Total
Advantage Healthplan		98		3,096				3,194
Aetna U.S. Healthcare	36,976	69					140,775	177,820
AMERIGROUP Maryland, Inc.				12,876				12,876
Capital Community Health Plan				28,851				28,851
CareFirst BlueChoice Inc.	39,708	417					6,409	46,534
Cigna Healthcare Mid-Atlantic, Inc.	1,654	1						1,655
DC Chartered Health Plan, Inc.	78	5		26,794				26,877
GHMSI	422,462	6,804			2,295	58,519	434,718	924,798
GW University Health Plan	49,034	719					33,101	82,854
Health Right, Inc.				9,168				9,168
Kaiser of the Mid-Atlantic	218,288	1,388	7,957			3,106	146,138	376,877
MD-IPA, Inc.	90,975						80,232	171,207
Optimum Choice	44,233							44,233
Prudential Health Care Plan, Inc.								0
United Healthcare of the Mid-Atlantic	1,279							1,279
Total	904,687	9,501	7,957	80,785	2,295	61,625	841,373	1,908,223

policies). Six health plans in D.C. offer a policy designed specifically for federal employees, but GHMSI alone holds 51.7 percent of the market.

Health Plan Enrollment by Product Type.   Managed-care companies typically offer several different health insurance products in the commercial group segment of the market. These products vary in terms of the health care providers that members may receive care from and who bears the risk that total premiums may not equal total expenses during the time the policy is in effect. At one end of the spectrum is the HMO product; for HMO policies, the managed-care company bears all the risk and members are restricted to a prespecified provider network.[14] At the other end of the spectrum is the indemnity product; for indemnity policies (which are rare today), the policyholder and the managed-care company jointly share risk up to some maximum benefit. Policyholders may receive care from any licensed provider.

Between these two extremes are preferred-provider-organization (PPO) products and point-of-service (POS) products. In both PPO and POS plans, the sponsoring managed-care company identifies a preferred list of providers. In the case of a POS, this preferred list of providers is usually the provider network for an HMO product; in the case of a PPO, the preferred providers have entered into contracts with the managed-care organization in which they have discounted the fees they charge. When a member of a PPO or a POS seeks care from a provider not included on the preferred provider list, the member is responsible for a co-insurance payment—a fixed percentage of the total amount that the nonpreferred provider charges the health plan for his or her services. When a member of a POS plan receives care from a preferred provider, there is typically no co-insurance payment. When a member of a PPO receives care from a preferred provider, there is typically a smaller co-insurance payment compared to the times when services are obtained from a nonpreferred provider. Because of differences in their provider networks and their benefit design, PPO products are imperfect substitutes for HMO products. Table 5.3 provides a brief description of different health insurance products.

Table 5.4 presents statistics on total health plan enrollment by product type in 2001 for health plans operating in D.C.[15] Approximately 71 percent of all health insurance products marketed by these health plans in the D.C.-Maryland-Virginia region are HMO products. The next largest category is the PPO product, which represents 21 percent of all health insurance products sold in this region by health plans that

Table 5.3
Descriptions of health insurance products as defined by InterStudy

Health insurance product	Description
Direct pay enrollment	Enrollees are individuals who are not members of a contracting group (i.e., they are enrolled under an individual coverage option).
FEHBP	Enrollees are federal employees and participate in the Federal Employees Health Benefits Program.
Commercial group	Includes individuals enrolled through employer-sponsored group HMO policies, as well as conversion members (persons who are no longer members of an employer group but under COBRA regulations are still eligible for HMO services at a group rate).
Public programs	Recipients of Medicaid and Medicare who are enrolled in an HMO.
Point of service (POS)	Enrollees have access to and financial incentives to use a managed-care provider network, often the HMO's provider panel, but in contrast to the open-panel HMO, POS enrollees are not prepaid enrollees of the HMO (they pay indemnity premiums).
Open-ended HMO	Enrollees are prepaid members of the HMO and may receive nonemergency services from providers outside the HMO's network. A substantial deductible, copayment, or need for coinsurance is usually required for use of nonpanel providers.
Preferred provider organization (PPO)	A fee-for-service product where beneficiaries receive care from a selected panel of providers. Providers agree to a discounted fee schedule when contracting with the PPO. PPOs offer a wide variety of benefit plans; some include the option of using nonpanel providers if beneficiaries pay out-of-pocket costs.
Managed fee for service (FFS)	The insurer pays the cost of covered services after services have been received and according to an agreed-on fee schedule. Various managed-care tools such as precertification, second surgical opinion, and utilization review are used.
Self-insured	The HMO providers deliver health services to an individual, but rather than being prepaid enrollees or premium paying beneficiaries, services received are paid for directly by the enrollee's employer.
Supplemental Medicare	A Medicare wraparound plan that covers some co-payments, deductibles, and services not covered under traditional Medicare. Beneficiaries are given financial incentives to use HMO providers but are not restricted to the HMO's panel.
Other non-HMO plans	This category primarily includes enrollees in flexcare plans, self-insured Medicare plans, managed indemnity, indemnity, exclusive provider organizations (EPOs), and out-of-area plans.

Table 5.4
Total regional health plan enrollment in 2001, by product type[a]

	HMO	PPO	POS	Indemnity	Total
Kaiser Foundation Health Plan	501,088		14,860		515,948
Prudential Health Care Plan	0				0
Health Right, Inc.	9,168				9,168
Optimum Choice, Inc.	392,153				392,153
MD-Individual Practice Assoc, Inc.	122,860				122,860
DC Chartered Health Plan	26,877				26,877
United Healthcare	180,478				180,478
Capital Community Health Plan	28,085				28,085
Amerigroup Maryland, Inc.	131,430				131,430
Aetna U.S. Healthcare, Inc.	369,004		36,396		405,400
Cigna Healthcare	32,589		4,485		37,074
GW University Health Plan	59,545		3,882		63,427
CareFirst BlueChoice	123,372		45,572		168,944
GHMSI		589,251	85,058	38,232	712,541
Advantage Healthplan, Inc.	3,194				3,194
Total	1,979,843	589,251	190,253	38,232	2,797,579

[a]Total health plan enrollment excluding FEHBP enrollment.

participate in the D.C. market. Note that all health plans offer an HMO product except for GHMSI, and that only GHMSI offers a PPO product or an indemnity product. GHMSI does not compete with any other managed-care firm in these two product markets and has the largest market share (approximately 45 percent) in the POS product market. CareFirst BlueChoice membership represents an additional 24 percent market share in the POS product market.

Market Concentration. Economists frequently employ the Herfindahl measure to quantify the extent to which market share is concentrated in a small number of firms. The Herfindahl concentration measure is computed as the sum of squared market shares for all firms in the mar-

ket. If there is only one firm in the market (i.e., a monopoly), the
Herfindahl statistic equals 1.0. If there are two firms of equal size in the
market, the Herfindahl statistic equals 0.5. Economists are interested in
market concentration because they believe it is related to a firm's bargaining power with suppliers and the ability of individual firms to
affect the price at which the market clears.

The Herfindahl statistic for the entire D.C. health insurance market
is 0.29, which is roughly equivalent to having three to four firms of
equal size in the market. In some more narrowly defined market segments, the Herfindahl statistics are substantially higher. For example,
the Herfindahl statistic in the individual market (policies sold to
individual consumers and not through a group purchaser) is 0.54;
GHMSI's share of this market is 72 percent. The Herfindahl statistic in
the FEHBP segment is 0.34, and GHMSI's market share is 52 percent. In
D.C., GHMSI is the only managed-care firm in the PPO and indemnity
market segments (Herfindahl = 1.0). Table 5.5 presents the Herfindahl
statistic and GHMSI's market share for each market segment in which
it participates.

Market Dynamics.   Point-in-time statistics on enrollment and market
share provide an incomplete picture of the competitive nature of a market. One might like to know which products, if any, have gained in

Table 5.5
Herfindahl statistics and GHMSI market share for market segments, 2001

Market segment	Herfindahl	GHMSI market share
Commercial Group	0.30	0.47
FEHBP	0.34	0.52
Individual	0.54	0.72
Medicare Supplemental	1.00	1.00
PPO	1.00	1.00
POS[a]	0.30	0.45
Indemnity	1.00	1.00

[a]Because enrollment by product type is reported only at the health plan level for the
entire D. C.-Maryland-Virginia market area, the Herfindal and GHMSI market share statistics are difficult to interpret. It is possible that managed-care companies offer POS
products in Maryland and Virginia but not in the District of Columbia. This situation
would cause the Herfindahl and GHMSI market share statistics in Table 5.4 to overstate
the true measures. Perhaps in the District, GHMSI is the only health plan offering a POS
product; in that case, the reported Herfindahl and GHMSI market share would underestimate the true measures.

popularity in recent years. Comparable historical data from health plan filings with the D.C. insurance commission were not available to construct a longtitudinal version of table 5.5. Enrollment by product type was available, however, from the InterStudy database for the years 1999 and 2001 for any health plan offering an HMO.[16]

Table 5.6 reports changes in the sum total of enrollment by product type for health plans that offer an HMO and whose primary service area is the District of Columbia, Maryland, or Virginia. These enrollment changes are also broken down by plan ownership type: national for-profit, Virginia Blue Cross Blue Shield, independent (includes for-profit and nonprofit), and CareFirst. A list of health plans in each ownership category is included in table 5.7.

The largest decreases in total enrollment marketwide occurred in the commercial group HMO product line and in the open-panel HMO product line. The largest increases occurred in PPO enrollment and enrollment in other non-HMO products. Data in table 5.6 suggest that the national for-profit firms decreased enrollment in commercial group HMO products and made up for about 83 percent of this HMO enrollment decrease with enrollment increases in PPO and other non-HMO

Table 5.6
Changes in enrollment by product type in the D.C.-Maryland-Virginia region, 1999–2001

	2001 Total enrollment	Enrollment change: 1999–2001				
		National for-profit	VA-BCBS	Independent	CareFirst	Total
Commercial						
HMO	1,759,586	−419,530	−28,726	−58,556	34,899	−471,913
PPO	645,149	101,435	0	−1,011	355,443	455,867
FEHBP	463,346	−13,142	1,746	15,714	−7,055	−2,737
Public	455,393	45,075	27,128	−3,425	−125,900	−57,122
Self	434,079	−137,959	0	−14,897	202,671	49,815
Open-Panel						
HMO	382,013	−111,823	−10,017	−3,728	−84,608	−210,176
Other						
non-HMO	275,474	245,378	0	26,306	0	271,684
POS	146,220	−45,365	0	0	0	−45,365
Direct	62,587	−9,927	−3,224	−2,445	−750	−16,346
FFS	0	0	0	0	0	0
Supplemental	0	0	0	0	0	0
Total						
managed care	4,626,062	−345,887	−13,093	−42,759	374,700	−27,039

Table 5.7
InterStudy health plans by ownership type in the D.C.-Maryland-Virginia market, 2001

National for-profit plans	Virginia: Blue Cross Blue Shield	Independent plans	CareFirst plans
United Healthcare of Mid-Atlantic	Healthkeepers	Kaiser of the Mid-Atlantic	FreeState HealthPlan
Aetna U.S. Healthcare (Maryland)	Peninsula Health Care	GW University Health Plan	Delmarva Health Plan
Prudential/Aetna (Virginia)	Priority Health Care	M.D.-IPA	CareFirst BlueChoice
CIGNA Healthcare of VA		OPTIMA Health Plan	PHN-HMO
Southern Health Services		QualChoice of Virginia	
CIGNA Healthcare of Mid-Atlantic		Optimum Choice	
Prudential/Aetna (Maryland)		Carilion Health Plans	
United Healthcare of VA		D.C. Chartered Health Plans	
AMERIGROUP (Maryland)		Piedmont Community HealthCare	
		Advantage Healthplan	
		Capital Community Health Plan	

products. Unlike other health plans in the D.C.-Maryland-Virginia market, CareFirst plans increased their commercial group HMO enrollment but decreased enrollment in all other HMO products. These decreases were more than offset, however, by large increases in PPO enrollment and enrollment in self-insured products.

Comparable nationwide enrollment changes between 1999 and 2001 are presented in table 5.8. Similarities between trends in the D.C.-Maryland-Virginia markets and nationwide include a substantial increase in PPO enrollment, a substantial decrease in commercial group and POS enrollment, and a decrease in nongroup direct enrollment products. In contrast to nationwide enrollment trends, total managed-care enrollment, FEHBP enrollment, and public program enrollment decreased in plans offering an HMO in the D.C.-Maryland-Virginia market, while they increased nationwide. Overall, however, it

Table 5.8
Enrollment changes nationwide, 1999–2001

	2001	Enrollment change: 1999–2001 (thousands)				
	Total enrollment (thousands)	National managed care	Not-for profit BCBS	For profit BCBS	Independent	Total
Commercial						
Group HMO	46,722	−4,429	73	1,384	−1,172	−4,144
PPO	36,324	4,376	817	6,917	2,289	14,399
FEHBP	2,362	−114	128	20	63	97
Public programs	17,746	−581	1,295	−1,002	1,174	886
Self-insured	6,759	−98	749	697	−280	1,068
Open-ended HMO	8,563	−164	14	257	−381	−273
Other non-HMO	6,879	3,108	575	115	427	4,225
POS	6,637	−895	−423	−1,640	111	−2,848
Direct pay	1,562	−256	114	−213	−121	−475
Managed FFS	2,334	−79	−107	900	309	1,023
Supplemental Medicare	1,040	− 21	305	445	73	803
Total managed care	137,998	858	3,631	7,917	2,619	15,025

seems that enrollment trends in the D.C.-Maryland-Virginia market area are similar to enrollment trends nationwide.

In summary, the market-share analysis indicates that the CareFirst plan, GHMSI, dominates the D.C. health insurance market. GHMSI has a large market share in the largest consumer segments. Furthermore, the markets in which GHMSI dominates are also concentrated. This combination suggests that GHMSI possesses market power in D.C. The next largest plan in the D.C. market is the Kaiser plan; note that the national for-profit health plans that CareFirst managers perceive as their primary competitors hold relatively small market shares in D.C. Because the market structure analyses were limited to the D.C. market, it is not possible to speculate whether other CareFirst plans possess similar favorable positions in the Maryland and Delaware markets.

National and local enrollment trends suggest a decline in traditional HMO and POS products and increases in PPO and other non-HMO products. CareFirst plans are at the forefront of this trend in the PPO market, but they lag behind the national for-profit firms in the market for other non-HMO products.

Economies of Scale. CareFirst executives and consultants have argued that the firm's acquisition by Wellpoint will lower CareFirst costs because of economies of scale. Strictly speaking, economies of scale are present when average unit costs fall with increased output. Average unit costs may decrease over some range of output for two reasons. First, large capital investments represent fixed costs that lead naturally to declining average costs up to some capacity constraint. Second, marginal costs may fall over some range of output because of learning curves, specialization, or volume discounts from suppliers.

In the health insurance market, economies of scale are present when the average total cost of insuring an individual is lower with high levels of total health plan enrollment than with low levels of total plan enrollment. Several intuitive reasons can explain why economies of scale might be present in managed-care operations. First, insurance is largely an information business and requires substantial capital investment in computers and software to manage that information. As long as the information systems are not at some capacity constraint, the information technology (IT) costs of processing information for an additional enrollee is essentially zero; hence, health plans can lower average costs by spreading these fixed costs of capital investment over a larger enrollment base. In a similar vein, health plans with a larger enrollment base may be able to support a larger Research and Development (R&D) group and have more opportunities for lower cost experimentation with new products and processes. Fixed costs are also associated with negotiating contracts with health care providers and purchasers.

Second, greater health plan enrollment may increase the bargaining power that the health plan can exercise in its negotiations over reimbursements with health care providers (e.g., doctors, hospitals, and pharmaceutical companies). The extent to which increased enrollment translates into greater bargaining power and lower medical-care costs (and hence lower average total costs) depends on local market characteristics. In markets where providers are themselves consolidated into large bargaining units or in which the demand for certain types of providers (e.g., high-quality teaching hospitals) is strong, the health plan's financial return to greater enrollment that derives from increased bargaining power is lower.

A third potential source of economies of scale in health insurance relates to the amount of financial reserves that a health plan must hold to meet statutory requirements. For statistical reasons, the per-enrollee amount of financial reserves that a health plan is required to hold is less for health plans with larger enrollment bases.

If we define economies of scale as average costs falling with increased enrollment, then it is possible to test for the presence of economies of scale in health insurance using a data set on health plan costs, enrollment, and other characteristics. The following paragraphs report the results of such an analysis.

Most states require health insurance plans to file quarterly and/or annual reports with the state insurance commissioner using a common format created by the National Association of Insurance Commissioners (NAIC). These data are publicly available. The Weiss Ratings Company collects and compiles these data and sells reports based on them. In the data compiled by the Weiss Ratings Company are reports of total health plan administrative expenditures, total health plan medical expenditures, total health plan enrollment, and several characteristics of the health plan and the insurance products it markets.

The sample for analysis was created by selecting all health plans classified as HMOs in the Weiss data reporting positive enrollment in 2001. These selection criteria yielded a sample size of 439 health plans. Health plans that enrolled Medicare beneficiaries (eleven plans) or Medicaid beneficiaries (sixty plans) exclusively were dropped from the analysis. Health plans reporting fewer than 5,000 enrollees (twenty-seven plans, five of which were Medicaid-only or Medicare-only plans) were also dropped from the sample. The remaining health plans were matched with the InterStudy database to collect additional information about the plans (321 matches out of the final Weiss sample of 347). Missing data for variables used as regressors led to a final sample size of 299 plans.

Figures 5.4 and 5.5 show substantial variation among health plans in administrative and medical expenses per member. The correlation between administrative and medical expenses is positive but not very large (correlation coefficient = 0.55). There is no reason to expect that economies of scale in administrative expenses would be the same as economies of scale in medical expenses. In fact, the earlier discussion suggests different sources of economies of scale in the two types of expenditures. For this reason, separate analyses were conducted to test

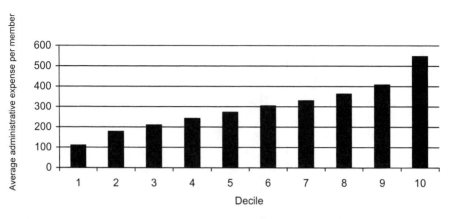

Figure 5.4
Average administrative expense

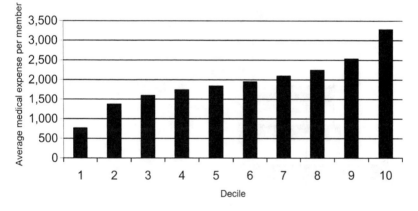

Figure 5.5
Average medical expense

for economies of scale in medical expenses and administrative expenses.

Figure 5.6 is a frequency distribution of health plan enrollment. This distribution is heavily skewed to the left; there is a relatively small number of plans with a very large enrollment (i.e., more than 500,000 enrollees). Note that 56 percent of health plans in this sample have HMO enrollment under 100,000 members (on the lower end of the plan size distribution). One indication of the presence of economies of scale is the distribution of medical and administrative expenses for health

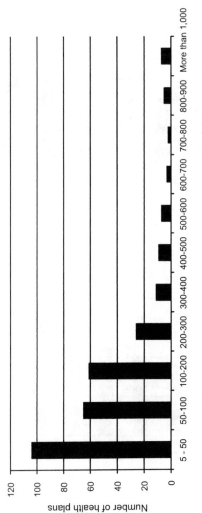

Figure 5.6
Expense deciles for plans in top enrollment decile

plans in the top enrollment decile. If economies of scale were present, one would expect to see an overrepresentation of these high-enrollment plans in the lowest deciles for average per-member medical and administrative expenses. Figure 5.7 suggests that this expectation is not the case; the high-enrollment plans are evenly represented in the administrative expense deciles and overrepresented in the higher medical expense deciles.

Figure 5.8 is a scatterplot of administrative expenses per member compared to health plan enrollment. Although many health plans are clustered in the low enrollment/low administrative expense quadrant of the graph, there does appear to be a negative relationship between average administrative expense and enrollment. In contrast, there appears to be no relationship discernible from the scatterplot of per-member medical expenses and enrollment (see figure 5.9).

Several health plan characteristics could influence average administrative and medical expenses independent of scale. Accounting practices in nonprofit health plans tend to result in a larger number of expenses classified as administrative compared to those in for-profit health plans. The average administrative and medical expenditures may differ by product line because of the variation in costs of delivering care to enrollees in different market segments. The InterStudy data records enrollment in several different product lines, including commercial HMO, FEHBP, Medicare risk HMO, Medicare supplemental,

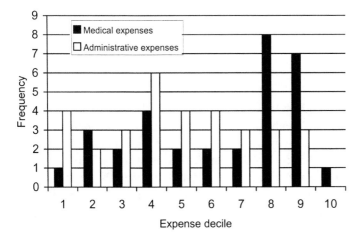

Figure 5.7
Expense deciles for plans in top enrollment decile

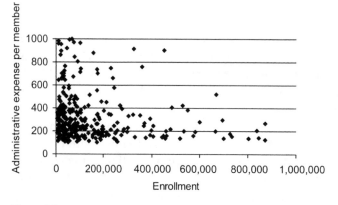

Figure 5.8
Plot of economies of scale in administrative expenses

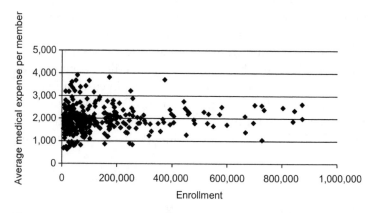

Figure 5.9
Plot of economies of scale in medical expenses

Medicaid risk HMO, POS, PPO, and FFS. In addition to the types of products offered by health plans, the total number of products may be positively related to average administrative costs. Because different product lines require product-specific investments in marketing, regulatory compliance, and provider networks, health plans concentrating their enrollment in fewer products are more likely to experience lower administrative expenses and possibly greater economies of scale.

Administrative and medical expenses per member may also be related to the health plan's provider network organization. There are four basic types of provider networks: (1) the staff model, in which physicians are employed by the health plan and are located in a small number of clinics; (2) the group model, in which health plans contract with physicians practicing in medical groups that may also contract with other health plans; (3) the Independent Physician Association (IPA) model, in which physicians in solo and group practice contract with an intermediary (the IPA), which in turn contracts with one or more health plans; and (4) the network model, in which health plans contract directly (not through an IPA) with a mix of solo-practice and group-practice physicians. Today, the provider networks of most health plans are a mix of these four model types. The organization of the health plan's provider network is related to, but not identical to, the breadth of the network (measured as the number of physicians per member). Health plans with predominantly IPA-based networks also tend to have larger networks.

Health plans contracting with a large number of providers for a given membership size will likely have larger administrative costs per member because of the additional transaction costs involved in negotiating and executing a larger number of contracts. It is also plausible that health plans with larger provider networks (controlling for membership size) will have higher medical expenses per member for three reasons: (1) adverse selection, (2) the health plan will find it more difficult to control utilization with a larger network and a smaller number of enrollees per provider, and (3) the health plan will be less able to negotiate lower provider reimbursement rates when providers see few of the plan's enrollees.

In addition to the network characteristics discussed in previous paragraphs, the method of provider payment may influence average administrative and medical costs. Consider two primary reimbursement methods: fee-for-service and capitation. Fee-for-service reimbursement requires the processing of a claim and payment on a claim to an individual physician every time a service is delivered. In contrast, capitation reimbursement sometimes involves no filing and processing of individual claims and only a monthly per-member payment to the physician or the practice. In some cases, health plans employing capitation require providers to submit dummy claims that the health plan then processes, but the health plan still makes payments less frequently. It is also likely that capitation reduces per-member medical costs.

In the last decade, there has been substantial consolidation of enrollment into a relatively small number of national and regional health plans. A statistical analysis of the relationship between local health plan enrollment and local health plan expenditures (both medical and administrative) that failed to account for affiliation with a national managed-care company might underestimate the true extent of economies of scale.[17] Affiliation with a national or regional managed-care company should convey economies of scale to a local plan to the extent that the cost of centralized services (i.e., claims processing) can be spread over a national or regional enrollment base.

Finally, a health plan's medical and administrative expenses may depend on the characteristics of the local health care markets in which it operates. There is substantial geographical variation in the organization of the provider sector, regulatory environment, and the extent of mandated benefits that could lead to differences in health plan cost structures.

Any one of these health plan or market characteristics could have an impact on average health plan administrative and medical expenditures. To assess empirically whether economies of scale exist in health plan enrollment, it is necessary to control statistically for these other factors. Consequently a regression analysis was undertaken to assess the relationship between health plan enrollment and average per-member administrative and medical expenses.

Table 5.9 presents the results of two regression analyses. In column 2, the dependent variable is administrative costs per member; in column 3, the dependent variable is average medical costs per member. A fixed effect for the health plan's primary state of operation (the state in which the health plan had the greatest enrollment) was included in each regression to control for regional variation in expenses. The estimated coefficients presented in columns 2 and 3 indicate that small but significant economies of scale are present in both administrative expenses and medical expenses. Because both the dependent variable and the enrollment variables are measured in natural logs, the coefficients on the enrollment variables in the regression may be interpreted as elasticities (e.g., the percentage change in administrative expenses associated with a one percentage change in enrollment). The estimated

Table 5.9
Economies of scale—regression results

Independent variable	Dependent variable log	
	Administrative expense per member	Medical expense per member
Percentage enrollment share—		
Medicare risk	[a]1.54 (0.22)	[a]1.78 (0.26)
Medicaid risk	[c]−0.28 (0.16)	−0.27 (0.18)
Direct pay	0.07 (0.41)	[a]−0.83 (0.28)
FEHBP	−0.25 (0.45)	0.14 (0.34)
Commercial HMO	−0.16 (0.14)	−0.30 (0.20)
POS	[a]0.74 (0.21)	[b]0.44 (0.22)
PPO	0.04 (0.14)	[c]−0.56 (0.29)
Supplemental Medicare	2.36 (1.75)	0.85 (0.97)
FFS	0.65 (0.55)	−0.29 (0.41)
Percentage provider payment—		
Capitation	−0.12 (0.14)	−0.12 (0.12)
Fee-for-service	0.05 (0.09)	−0.03 (0.13)
Provider payment imputation	[c]−0.31 (0.19)	−0.31 (0.24)
Product Herfindahl	0.12 (0.18)	0.28 (0.20)
Age of plan	0.00 (0.00)	0.00 (0.00)
Physicians per 1,000 enrollees	[a]475.34 (152.54)	[a]−796.89 (208.74)
Log of enrollment	[b]−0.05 (0.03)	[b]−0.64 (0.03)
Log of national managed-care enrollment	−0.00 (0.01)	0.00 (0.00)
Log of regional managed-care enrollment	0.00 (0.01)	−0.01 (0.01)
For-profit HMO	[b]0.16 (0.08)	−0.01 (0.06)
Percentage of enrollment in IPA or mixed model	[b]0.14 (0.06)	[b]0.13 (0.06)
Number of products	0.00 (0.02)	[a]0.07 (0.02)
Number of states	0.13 (0.11)	0.15 (0.14)
Constant	[a]5.82 (0.29)	[a]7.85 (0.29)
State dummy variables	Included	Included
Number of observations	299	299
R-squared	0.50	0.54

[a] $p \leq 0.01$.
[b] $p \leq 0.05$.
[c] $p \leq 0.10$.
Note: Standard errors in parentheses.

coefficient on within-plan enrollment is –0.05 for administrative expenses and –0.06 for medical expenses, indicating that a one percentage increase in the health plan's enrollment is associated with a .05 to .06 percentage point decrease in average administrative and medical costs, respectively. These estimated relationships are depicted in figures 5.10 and 5.11.

Recall that, for plans affiliated with national or regional managed-care companies, the total national or regional enrollment was entered

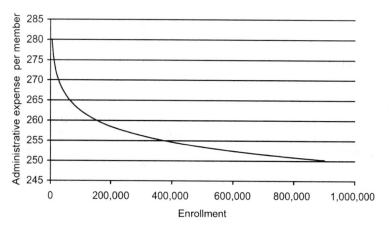

Figure 5.10
Estimated economies of scale in administrative expenditures

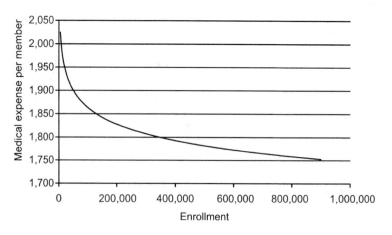

Figure 5.11
Estimated economies of scale in medical expenses

separately into the regression. The coefficients on these variables indicate the extent to which the additional scale (enrollment) present in a national or regional managed-care company is associated with higher or lower administrative expenses per member in the local plan. The point estimates on these enrollment variables in both regressions are essentially zero and insignificant.

Given the topic of this paper, it is worthwhile to note that this regression analysis suggests that nonprofit health plans have significantly higher per-member administrative costs but not significantly different average medical costs. As noted earlier, however, this finding may be an artifact of nonprofit accounting customs.

In summary, the regression analysis finds evidence of modest economies of scale in both administrative and medical costs. The estimated economies of scale are nearly exhausted at an enrollment of roughly 800,000. Only twelve health plans in our sample have an enrollment greater than this number. In addition, it appears that there are no additional economies of scale to be gained through membership in a regional or national managed-care company.

Quality of Care. Consumers, providers, managers, and researchers all acknowledge that quality in health care is multidimensional and difficult to measure. These characteristics of quality lead to difficulties in contracting for a specified level of quality and to challenges in holding individuals and organizations accountable for the quality of health care services delivered. Quality of care arises as an issue in health plan conversions because of the potential opportunity and financial incentive for a for-profit health plan to skimp on the aspects of quality that are difficult for consumers to observe and verify.

Differences in quality between health plans do exist and are sometimes large. For example, the Centers for Disease Control estimates that nearly 16 million Americans have diagnosed or undiagnosed diabetes. If not properly managed, diabetes can have devastating health consequences and can consume lots of expensive health care resources. To manage their disease, people with diabetes and their physicians must know the level of the patient's hemoglobin A1c (HbA1c), and this information is obtained through a simple blood test. In the sample of plans reporting data to the National Committee on Quality Assurance in 2000, the percentage of diabetic plan members who had their HbA1c tested ranged from 24 percent to 97 percent. This range suggests substantial variation in performance and ample room for improvement.

Research has shown that health plans that undertake diabetes disease management programs can effect substantial improvements in care and short-term outcomes for people with diabetes.

Published health services research documents correlations between health plan performance on some quality measures and various health plan characteristics.[18] Although the root causes of these patterns are not well understood, local independent and nonprofit health plans frequently outperform for-profit, publicly traded, national managed-care plans. These findings are important for public officials to consider as they determine whether particular conversions are in the interest of health care consumers. In the following section, I compare the performance of CareFirst, Wellpoint, and other health plans operating in their respective markets on various measures of health plan quality.

Measures of Health Plan Quality. In 1997, the National Committee on Quality Assurance (NCQA) began reporting the performance of some health plans on a selected set of quality measures. This set of measures (the Health plan and Employers Data Information Set [HEDIS]) was chosen by a group of health care purchasers and medical professionals and has been expanded over the years. Health plans voluntarily submit performance data (most is audited) to the NCQA, which then publishes these data in a product called Quality Compass. Consumers and employers have used these data to help them make health care purchasing decisions; academic researchers have used these data to study the causes of variation in health plan quality.

The HEDIS measures convey information about the extent to which the health plan's enrollees are obtaining preventive services and diagnostic tests necessary for managing certain chronic diseases. (See table 5.10 for a list of HEDIS measures used in the analyses presented in this paper.) The HEDIS set also includes a few measures of health care

Table 5.10
Definitions of HEDIS quality measures

Adolescent immunization rates	Estimates the percentage of adolescent health plan members that have been verified to have received all required doses of several vaccines by their thirteenth birthday.
Rate of advising smokers to quit	Measures the percentage of eligible health plan members who were advised to quit smoking during a visit with a physician during the measurement year.

Table 5.10
(continued)

Use of appropriate medications for people with asthma	Evaluates whether health plan members who are suffering from persistent asthma are being prescribed medications deemed acceptable by the National Heart, Lung and Blood Institute as primary therapy for long-term control of asthma.
Beta blocker treatment after a heart attack	Estimates the percentage of members age 35 and older who are hospitalized and discharged from the hospital after surviving a heart attack (defined as an acute myocardial infarction [AMI]) and who received a prescription for a beta blocker.
Breast cancer screening rates	Estimates the percentage of women age 52 through 69 who are enrolled in a health plan and who had a mammogram during the measurement year or the year prior to the measurement year.
Cervical cancer screening rates	Estimates the percentage of women age 21 to 64 who were enrolled in a health plan and who had an Papanicolau (Pap) test during the measurement year or the two years prior.
Childhood immunization rates	Estimates the percentage of children who were enrolled in managed-care plans, turned two years old during the measurement year, and had received vaccinations: (1) four doses of DTP or DtaP (diptheria-tetanus), (2) three doses of OPV or IPV (polio), (3) one dose of MMR (measles-mumps-rubella), (4) two doses of Hib (Haemophilus influenza), (5) three doses of Hepatitis B, and (6) one dose of VZV (chicken pox).
Chlamydia screening rates	Estimates the percentage of sexually active female plan members who had at least one test for chlamydia during the measurement year. The measure is collected separately for women age 16 to 20 and 21 to 26.
Comprehensive diabetes care	Measure set includes several important features of effective, multphasic management of diabetes and its complications. The measure estimated the percentage of health plan members with Type 1 and Type 2 diabetes who were 18 to 75 years old and during the measurement year had (1) a hemoglobin A1c (HbA1c) test, (2) poorly controlled HbA1c (level greater that 9.5%), (3) a serum cholesterol level (LDL-C) screening, (4) their cholesterol level (LDL-C) controlled to less than 130 mg/dl, (5) an eye exam, and (6) a screening for kidney disease.
Follow-up after mental illness, 7-day and 30-day rates	Indicates the percentage of health plan members age six and older who received inpatient treatment for a mental health disorder and had an ambulatory or day/night follow-up visit after being discharged.
Prenatal and postpartum care rates	Measures timeliness of prenatal care and postpartum care.

outcomes for the health plan's enrolled population that signal how well
the health plan is doing overall at helping its members stay healthy.

The second set of measures of health plan quality is derived from a
survey instrument called the Consumer Assessment of Health Plans
Survey (CAHPS); CAHPS data are included in Quality Compass. The
survey is administered by an independent party to a random sample of
the health plan's enrollees to collect data on consumers' experiences in
seeking and obtaining health care. Health plans often submit their performance on CAHPS to organizations that publish comparative health
plan data (such as the federal government, the NCQA, and local health
care purchasing groups). The federal government has mandated the
collection and reporting of these survey data for Medicare beneficiaries
enrolled in Medicare HMOs.

The CAHPS instrument generates hard-to-find data on the quality of
enrollees' interactions with providers and health plans. (See Table 5.11
for a list of CAHPS measures used in the analyses presented in this
report.) Health plans can take many actions to facilitate consumers'
access to care, to educate consumers about and involve them in their
own health care, to ease the administrative burden of dealing with
insurance claims, and to select and support a provider network that
routinely delivers high-quality patient-friendly care. The CAHPS
measures provide health plans with an opportunity to distinguish
themselves in these areas.

HEDIS Comparisons. CareFirst operates three separate health plans in
the mid-Atlantic region that reported 1999 HEDIS data to NCQA (the
data are published in Quality Compass 2000): CapitalCare Inc.,
Delmarva Health Plan Inc., and FreeState Health Plan Inc. In the analyses that follow, an average score is computed for all three CareFirst
plans weighted by HMO enrollment. Wellpoint operates the Blue Cross
of California (BC-CA) health plan in California; this plan reported a
limited set of 1999 HEDIS data to NCQA. Performance on HEDIS
measures may be influenced by some factors beyond the health plan's
control, such as sociodemographic characteristics of the plan's membership, local organization of providers, and state health initiatives. To
control for variation in some of these factors across markets, the HEDIS
scores of each plan have been adjusted for the region of the country in
which the health plan operates.

Table 5.12 presents HEDIS data comparing the average performance
of the CareFirst plans to Wellpoint's California plan and to the national

Table 5.11
Definitions of CAHPs quality measures

Getting care quickly	Measures timeliness of services received from health care providers in the last twelve months.
Claims processing	Measures managed-care enrollees' experiences with submitting claims to their health plans in the last twelve months.
Customer service	Measures how difficult it was for enrollees in managed care plans to obtain information and to complete paperwork in the last twelve months.
How well doctors communicate	Measures the consumers' experiences while seeing a doctor or health care provider in the last twelve months.
Getting needed care	A composite measure consisting of several questions related to consumers' experiences in attempting to obtain care from doctors and specialists.
Courtesy of office staff	Measures managed-care enrollees' perception of quality of customer service when interacting with staff in their doctors' offices and clinics in the last twelve months.
Overall rating of doctor	Respondents were asked to rate their personal doctor or nurse with 0 ("worst personal doctor or nurse possible") to 10 ("best personal doctor or nurse possible").
Overall rating of specialist	Respondents who had seen a specialist physician in the last twelve months were asked to rate their specialist with 0 ("worst specialist possible") to 10 ("best specialist possible").
Overall rating of health plan	Respondents were asked to rate their health plan with 0 ("worst health plan possible") to 10 ("best health plan possible").
Overall rating of health care	Respondents were asked to rate the quality of the health care they received in the last twelve months, with 0 ("worst health care possible") to 10 ("best health care possible").

average on three types of measures: preventive care, chronic care, and mental health care. CareFirst performs least well on the preventive-care measures; its scores exceed the national average on four out of ten measures, and BC-CA outperforms CareFirst on six out of the seven measures for which data were submitted by BC-CA. The second group of measures relates to care for enrollees with chronic disease. BC-CA reported only one out of eight measures in this group, and its performance on this measure falls significantly below CareFirst's performance. CareFirst outperforms the national average on six out of eight measures in the chronic-care category. Finally, in the third group of measures relating to mental health care, CareFirst outperforms BC-CA on the two measures for which Wellpoint submitted data. CareFirst outperformed the national average on three out of five measures in this category.

Table 5.12
Comparison of CareFirst and Wellpoint plans on HEDIS measures

HEDIS measures	CareFirst	BC-CA	National	National Public FP	National standard deviation
Preventive care					
Child immunization 1	77.6	68.4	65.9	65.7	13.0
Child immunization 2	65.6		48.7	47.6	11.7
Adol immunization 1	24.7	27.4	33.2	28.7	17.7
Adol immunization 2	16.7		15.6	12.4	11.9
Advice to quit smoking	70.1	60.8	64.7	62.3	6.9
Breast cancer screening	70.6	75.9	74.9	72.6	5.9
Cervical cancer screening	68.4	70.1	73.7	71.8	7.7
Prenatal care	85.1	87.3	86.4	86.8	11.1
Checkup after delivery	69.3	79.1	74.6	73.7	11.8
Beta blockers	85.5	86.9	86.5	87.2	9.7
Chronic care					
Cholesterol rate	18.8		47.8	45.1	15.0
Cholesterol screening	70.7		70.2	67.8	11.1
HbA1c test	79.1		77.3	76.3	8.9
Diabetic eye exam	58.8	39.5	48.5	44.7	14.3
Lipid profile	68.0		70.4	69.7	9.9
Lipid control	44.8		38.6	35.8	9.6
Nephropathy monitoring	38.1		37.3	35.7	14.4
HbA1c control	79.7		58.0	55.3	14.3
Mental health care					
Mental illness—7 days	60.6	45.0	49.2	49.6	14.7
Mental illness—30 days	72.0	50.5	72.3	70.9	13.7
Depression contact	8.7		21.3	19.9	10.3
Depression, acute	68.9		60.3	61.3	9.5
Depression, continuous	45.2		43.6	43.2	10.4

These comparisons between the CareFirst plans and the Wellpoint-CA plan suggest that each of these plans has strengths and weaknesses and that neither plan dominates the other on HEDIS measures. Note that at least one CareFirst plan reported data for every HEDIS measure (twenty-three measures in all), while the Wellpoint-CA plan reported data on just less than half of the measures. The collection and public reporting of plan performance on HEDIS measures signals a plan's commitment to improving health care quality.

Table 5.13 facilitates a comparison of performance by CareFirst and Wellpoint-CA on HEDIS measures to the Kaiser plans operating in the CareFirst and Wellpoint-CA markets. The Kaiser Foundation is the holding company for the only truly national, nonprofit, managed-care

Table 5.13
Comparison of BCBS plans to Kaiser plans on HEDIS measures

	CareFirst	Kaiser Mid-Atlantic	BC-CA	Kaiser California
Preventive care				
Child immunization 1	77.6	88.6	68.4	76.2
Child immunization 2	65.6	76.5		69.5
Adol immunization 1	24.7	48.4	27.4	34.5
Adol immunization 2	16.7	50.2		16.6
Advice to quit smoking	70.1	67.6	60.8	68.0
Breast cancer screening	70.6	79.4	75.9	75.8
Cervical cancer screening	68.4	88.6	70.1	77.4
Prenatal care	85.1	86.9	87.3	89.5
Check-up after delivery	69.3	80.1	79.1	83.2
Beta blockers	85.5	98.3	86.9	89.7
Chronic care				
Cholesterol rate	18.8	67.5		45.2
Cholesterol screening	70.7	75.3		78.4
HbA1c test	79.1	85.9		77.5
Diabetic eye exam	58.8	87.7	39.5	64.0
Lipid profile	68.0	69.2		70.5
Lipid control	44.8	41.9		41.2
Nephropathy monitoring	38.1	74.8		55.2
HbA1c control	79.7	71.1		55.1
Mental health care				
Mental illness—7 days	60.6	65.5	45.0	62.6
Mental illness—30 days	72.0	79.2	50.5	83.3
Depression contact	8.7	34.6		28.4
Depression, acute	68.9	63.8		68.6
Depression, continuous	45.2	46.1		58.2

plan in the United States. All other nonprofit managed-care companies have only a local or a regional presence. The Kaiser Foundation plans in California and the mid-Atlantic region reported a full set of 1999 HEDIS data to NCQA.

Comparing the second and third columns of table 5.13, note that Kaiser of the Mid-Atlantic outperforms CareFirst on nearly every HEDIS measure (nineteen out of twenty-three). Second, comparing the third and fourth columns of the table, note that the Kaiser plans of California outperform Wellpoint on nearly every measure for which Wellpoint reported data (ten out of eleven). Finally, Kaiser Mid-Atlantic outperforms Kaiser California on sixteen out of the twenty-three measures. This comparison of the two Kaiser plans raises the concern that the method used for controlling for systematic geographical variation was not completely successful. However, the magnitude of the differences between the Kaiser plans and CareFirst and Wellpoint plans suggests systematic differences even within a region.

In summary, three major conclusions emerge from these comparisons on HEDIS measures. First, the CareFirst and the BC-CA plans each have strengths and weaknesses on HEDIS measures, and neither plan dominates the other. BC-CA compares favorably on preventive-care measures, while the CareFirst plans compare favorably on chronic-care and mental-health-care measures. Second, both the BC–CA plan and the CareFirst plans are outperformed by the Kaiser plans in their respective markets on HEDIS measures.

CAHPS comparisons. This section of the report presents comparisons of the performance of several health plans on the set of CAHPS composite measures published in Quality Compass 2000. Examination of table 5.14 shows that the CareFirst plans outperform the BC-CA plan on eight out of ten CAHPS measures (the plans are essentially equal on two measures). The largest differences between the health plans' performance relate to access to care—getting care quickly and getting needed care. Table 5.13 also facilitates a comparison of the BC-CA and CareFirst plans to the national average. BC-CA performs below the

Table 5.14
Comparison of CareFirst and Wellpoint plans on CAHPS measures

	CareFirst	BC-CA	National	National Public FP	National standard deviation
Claims processing	83.0	81.1	79.1	76.4	9.2
Courteous staff	90.7	88.8	91.6	90.7	2.7
Customer service	66.0	64.9	65.8	63.0	6.3
Getting care quickly	78.1	67.6	79.2	77.8	5.4
Getting needed care	77.2	70.6	75.4	72.7	6.8
Communication with doctor	91.2	86.2	89.8	88.9	2.9
Overall health care rating	68.5	68.4	71.1	68.8	6.1
Overall health plan rating	59.2	56.0	58.0	53.5	8.4
Overall PCP rating	74.0	74.2	73.5	73.2	4.4
Overall specialist rating	75.5	67.4	75.3	74.6	4.8

national average on eight out of ten CAHPS measures; CareFirst performs better than the national average on seven out of ten measures. Also note that the average for national, publicly traded, for-profit health plans is below the average for all plans nationally.

The Kaiser Mid-Atlantic plan outperforms the CareFirst plans on two out of the ten CAHPS measures, in contrast, the Kaiser California plan outperforms the BC-CA plan on nine out of ten measures (see table 5.15).

In summary, the analysis of CAHPS quality measures suggests that CareFirst members have had more favorable experiences in obtaining health care services compared to the Wellpoint plan in California. Comparisons to local Kaiser plans in each market reinforce the findings of the head-to-head comparison of BC-CA and the CareFirst plans.

Postscript in the CareFirst Conversion Case

The Maryland insurance commissioner, Stephen Larsen, initiated hearings on CareFirst's conversion petition prior to the insurance commissioners in the District of Columbia and Delaware. As part of the Maryland hearings and in anticipation of formal hearings in D.C., several consultants were hired to value CareFirst; most of these valuations exceeded Wellpoint's offer of $1.3 billion. In the course of the hearings, concerns were also raised about the process used by the board of

Table 5.15
Comparison of CareFirst and Wellpoint plans to Kaiser plans on CAHPS measures

	Care-First	Kaiser Mid-Atlantic	BC-CA	Kaiser California
Claims processing	83.0	66.0	81.1	79.1
Courteous staff	90.7	90.5	88.8	90.3
Customer service	66.0	77.4	64.9	73.0
Getting care quickly	78.1	80.0	67.6	76.0
Getting needed care	77.2	76.2	70.6	78.8
Communication with doctor	91.2	82.2	86.2	87.0
Overall health care rating	68.5	65.2	68.4	70.3
Overall health plan rating	59.2	57.3	56.0	64.5
Overall PCP rating	74.0	72.4	74.2	75.0
Overall specialist rating	75.5	71.3	67.4	75.3

CareFirst to solicit bids and the board's selection of the Wellpoint offer. Finally, the terms of the deal appeared to enrich CareFirst executives personally.

On March 5, 2003, Commissioner Larson denied the petition by CareFirst to convert to for-profit status and to be acquired by Wellpoint. Both the District of Columbia and Delaware suspended their conversion proceedings. In reviewing the research and evidence, Commissioner Larson found three reasons to deny the conversion. First, he found that CareFirst had been operating like a for-profit company despite legal requirements to adhere to a nonprofit, public-interest mission. Second, he found that the CareFirst board failed to consider CareFirst's obligations as a nonprofit entity, and that the board did not negotiate the best price for CareFirst and was offering to sell at less than fair market value. Third, and finally, Commissioner Larson found that CareFirst did not demonstrate a need to convert to for-profit status to remain viable.

On April 8, 2003, the Maryland legislature ratified Larsen's decision and passed Senate bill 772. In essence, the bill is an attempt to restructure CareFirst as a functioning nonprofit health plan that will execute its mission. It calls for replacement of all Maryland-appointed CareFirst board members and compensation to be paid to board members, officers and employees to be comparable to similar positions in other nonprofit organizations. It establishes a joint nonprofit health service plan oversight committee to oversee CareFirst operations in a manner consistent with the interests of Maryland citizens, and it prohibits the acquisition of CareFirst for five years. In terms of health plan conduct, it requires that CareFirst (1) offer health care products in the individual and small-group markets, (2) administer and subsidize the Senior Prescription Drug Program in Maryland, and (3) devote any remaining avoided taxes to a public-interest project.

Far from closing the chapter on CareFirst's petition to convert, the Maryland legislation sparked controversy in the District of Columbia and action by some of the parties. The D.C. insurance commissioner claimed that the Maryland legislation could render the CareFirst plan in D.C. uncompetitive and not viable. The Blue Cross and Blue Shield Association revoked CareFirst's use of the BCBS brand. Finally, Wellpoint abandoned hopes of acquiring CareFirst and announced a deal to acquire the publicly traded holding company of BCBS of Wisconsin.